To

Mary J.

Be Happy

Be Healthy

Be Well!

Love

[signature]

LAURA THEODORE'S

vegan-ease

AN *EASY* GUIDE TO ENJOYING A PLANT-BASED DIET

JAZZY VEGETARIAN, LLC

Library of Congress Cataloging-in-Publication Data

Theodore, Laura.
  Laura Theodore's VEGAN-*EASE* : An *Easy* Guide to Enjoying a Plant-Based Diet / Laura Theodore.
    p. cm.
  ISBN **978-0-9965475-0-5** (hardcover)
1. Vegan cooking.   2. Vegan lifestyle.   3. Cookbooks.   4. Title.

Front cover photo: David Kaplan
Interior and back cover photos: David Kaplan, Laura Theodore,
    Andy Ebberbach, Jacob Fisher
*Photos on pages 6, 51, 115, 122, 125, 132, and 167 by Annie Oliverio
*Photo on page 162 by Hannah Kaminsky

Editor: Kit Emory
Proofreader: Karen L. Stein
Nutritional Analysis Provided by: Mitali Shah-Bixby, MS, RD, CSSD, LDN

Cover and Interior Design: John Wincek, Aerocraft Charter Art Service

Hair Styling and Make Up: Amy Marie McGowan
Hair Design: Kym Rebelo
Dinnerware for Photos Provided by: Cardinal International

Jazzy Vegetarian

Jazzy Vegetarian, LLC
P.O. Box 313
Bloomingdale, NJ 07403
www.jazzyvegetarian.com
www.lauratheodore.com

PRINTED IN THE UNITED STATES

10 9 8 7 6 5 4 3 2 1

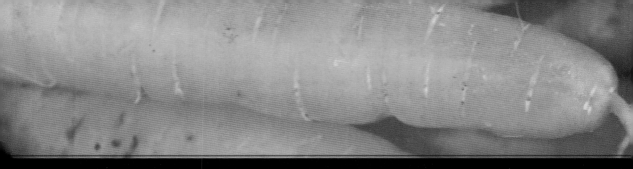

"*The doctor of the future will give no medicine, but will interest his patients in the care of the human frame, in diet, and in the cause and prevention of disease.*"

THOMAS A. EDISON

contents

foreword

When something comes along that seamlessly meets a widespread need—luggage with wheels did that; so did noise-canceling headphones—I always think, *"This should have been around forever."*

I feel the same way about Laura Theodore's enchanting new cookbook, Vegan-*Ease*. Giving each recipe an "Ease-Factor"? How brilliant is *that*?! And letting the cook—that's you or me—choose how much salt and pepper to add, based on our own needs and preferences? Very nice. How about providing tips that are new to even a longtime vegan like myself? Cutting edge. (I didn't know until reading this book to store brown rice in the refrigerator, and I've been eating brown rice since people went to San Francisco with flowers in their hair.)

It seems to me that the user-friendliness of this book has two sources. First is real life. Laura moved from Manhattan (where you can get anything at any time and have it delivered) to the country, where one gets clean air and natural beauty. But a 24-hour organic market? Not on your life. Instead of complaining or settling for packaged and processed foods, Laura went for the superfoods—*i.e.*, plants, lots of colors—available in her local supermarket. Her enlightened brand of "making do" means that we get to make the impressive dishes described in these pages. (And if the recipe that garners the biggest compliments has an Ease-Factor of "1," well, surely some things can be kept private.)

The other source of this book's charm and functionality is its author herself. Laura Theodore is an artist on many fronts: a singer, TV and radio host, and culinary creative who can transform simple ingredients into simply stunning cuisine. Use these recipes and notice your palate favoring foods that are honest and beautiful. Watch your health improve and your outlook become more positive. And pay particular attention to the way your heart opens up when you're no longer eating animals. It's a sweet, subtle shift that will make you feel really good—about yourself and about your dinner.

Victoria Moran
author of *Main Street Vegan* and *The Good Karma Diet*

JAZZY VEGETARIAN GRATEFULLY THANKS AND ACKNOWLEDGES OUR SEASON FIVE SPONSORS, **QUAKER, VITAMIX,** AND **PASCHA CHOCOLATE,** WHOSE GENEROUS SUPPORT HAS MADE IT POSSIBLE TO SHARE THESE RECIPES WITH THE WORLD.

JAZZY VEGETARIAN GRATEFULLY ACKNOWLEDGES OUR PAST SPONSORS, **TROPICANA** AND **DAWN.**

introduction

Making the World a Better Place, One Vegan Recipe at a Time.

Twelve years ago, when my husband Andy and I moved from the hustle and bustle of New York City to a beautiful lakeside community in northern New Jersey, I quickly discovered that vegan restaurants in my neighborhood were not to be found. Tiring of the pasta dishes at the local Italian eatery and not wanting to drive ten miles for a macrobiotic plate in another town, I needed to find a better solution. I wanted to create tasty plant-based meals at home that could be put together quickly and easily. But this was more of a challenge than I'd bargained for, due to the limited selection of organic fresh produce and quality plant-powered protein locally available.

New York had spoiled me with its plentiful vegan eateries. Plus, there were so many fantastic markets nearby, all I had to do was walk a couple of blocks and I had every fresh organic fruit and vegetable I could want at my fingertips. In addition to all the fabulous produce available, I had no trouble finding all sorts of enticing plant-based protein sources to anchor my recipes. Needless to say, it was easy for this passionate foodie to prepare all sorts of delectable vegan dishes in my little closet of a kitchen (really, it had once been a closet!) and nothing stopped me from going where my culinary inspiration took me.

Who knew that garden fresh, organically grown produce would be hard to come by in my newly adopted Garden State, even during the few short months at the peak of summer?

So I said to myself: *What's a veggie-loving vegan to do?*

Quickly taking culinary matters into my own hands, I started to transform many of my family's classic recipes, along with some of my own creations, into easy-to-prepare vegan dishes using ingredients that I could locate at my neighborhood New Jersey supermarket. Focusing on local and seasonal produce while cultivating my own little garden of potted herbs and leafy greens on my back deck each summer, I began to redefine the process of creating daily meals. Entertaining my omnivorous friends and family was the next step! Cooking for—*and pleasing*—meat-eaters proved to be particularly challenging but I was determined to find delicious and satisfying alternatives for my guests.

Then it dawned on me: If *I* was having a difficult time creating tasty and easy vegan meals from the narrow assortment of organic produce and animal-free protein sources obtainable in my new home town, what about everyone *else* in small towns across America trying to make healthy meals at home?

Soon I found myself on a culinary mission to reinvent and redefine how to create and serve simple, tasty meals, employing basic ingredients that could easily be purchased locally. This is the essence of Vegan-*Ease*.

It took a lot of hard work and experimenting, but I've never looked back. I'm proud of the results, lovingly tested on family, friends and neighbors—omnivores, vegetarians and vegans alike. In the pages of this book, I joyfully present to you my Vegan-*Ease* recipes, all designed to make your healthy meals divinely delicious and easy. I hope you will love these recipes as much as I do.

Thank you for joining me on this empowering journey of a lifetime.

Happy, healthy cooking!

Laura Theodore

PART I

what do I eat *and why?*

making vegan easy

Facing page: Roasted Cauliflower Cutlets with Lemon-Caper Sauce, page 124

2

hat makes a vegan recipe healthy, tasty *and* easy? Vegan-*Ease*!

A plant-based diet is a healthy, compassionate and "eco-nomical" way to eat, incorporating diverse and delicious ingredients. In the pages of this book we'll explore tasty food, focusing on fresh produce and easy-to-find pantry staples. Vegan-*Ease* transforms universally popular dishes by using minimally processed plant-based ingredients that result in a delicious, healthier version of the original recipe.

Vegan-*Ease* Defined

According to the Merriam-Webster dictionary, a *vegan* is "a strict vegetarian who consumes no animal food or dairy products; also: one who abstains from using animal products (as leather)."[1] According to the same dictionary, the word *ease* encompasses "freedom from pain or trouble," "comfort of body or mind" as well as "lack of difficulty."[2]

The phrase Vegan-*Ease* combines the terms "vegan" and "ease" to describe simple plant-based recipes, using readily available ingredients that are animal-free.

All of the recipes in this cookbook are designed to help you easily incorporate delicious, plant-based recipes into your weekly menu plan. Lovingly created in the Jazzy Vegetarian (vegan) kitchen, the recipes are geared toward omnivores, vegetarians and long-time vegans alike and are suitable for novice cooks.

Recipes Made *Ease-y*

All of the recipes in this book contain:

EASE-Y **to find ingredients** that can be purchased at your local supermarket or health food store. In a few cases you may need to buy online.

EASE-Y **to prepare dishes** that save time in the kitchen and provide tasty and nutritious meals for you and your family.

EASE-Y **on the wallet menus** that often incorporate local and seasonal produce along with cost-saving vegan protein sources to help you save dollars on your weekly grocery bill.

EASE-Y **on the earth meals** that support a healthier global environment, conserving resources like our water supply, while decreasing our individual carbon footprint.

EASE-Y **to eat foods** that will please your palate and satisfy deliciously!

Vegan-Ease: Good for the environment, your body and your budget!

Ease-Factor

We have ranked each recipe with an "Ease-Factor" to make it simpler for you to choose recipes that work within your schedule and facilitate planning your daily meals.

EASE-FACTOR ❶

This recipe is quick and easy to prepare, has up to 7 ingredients (not inclusive of water, salt or pepper). It takes fewer than 15 minutes to be ready to serve, refrigerate, or prepare for the oven, and incorporates foods that are readily available at any well-stocked supermarket.

EASE-FACTOR ❷

This recipe has up to 10 ingredients (not inclusive of water, salt or pepper). It takes fewer than 30 minutes to be ready to serve, refrigerate, or prepare for the oven, and incorporates ingredients that are generally available at any well-stocked supermarket or reputable health food store.

EASE-FACTOR ❸

This recipe has up to 15 ingredients (not inclusive of water, salt or pepper). It takes more than 30 minutes to be ready to serve, refrigerate, or prepare for the oven, and incorporates ingredients that are mostly available at any well-stocked supermarket or reputable health food store.

Look for the Ease-Factor in each recipe when shopping for—or preparing—your daily meals.

NOTES

[1] http://www.merriam-webster.com/dictionary/vegan

[2] http://www.merriam-webster.com/dictionary/ease

- A sturdy pair of large, stainless-steel tongs
- Wire whisks in several sizes
- A measuring cup and measuring spoon set
- Several sizes of stainless steel bowls for mixing, cooking, serving and storing

CUTTING BOARDS

- A small-sized board (ideal for smaller chopping chores)
- A large board (for cutting large bunches of greens as well as bigger vegetables and fruits)

SPINNERS AND STRAINERS

- A salad spinner (crisp green salads start with washed greens that are spun dry)
- Large and medium colanders for draining pasta and cleaning produce
- A set of small-screened strainers in various sizes, for rinsing grains and other small ingredients before cooking

STAINLESS STEEL OR NONREACTIVE POTS AND PANS

- A small and medium-sized saucepan (with steamer basket to fit), both with fitted lids
- One sauté pan or skillet with lid
- A large soup pot with lid

TOOLS, UTENSILS AND GADGETS

- Box grater
- Carrot peeler
- Citrus squeezer or lemon reamer
- Grapefruit spoon
- Lemon zester
- Pastry brush
- Potato masher
- Vegetable-cleaning brush
- Hot pads or potholders *(a MUST for handling hot food safely!)*

VEGAN-*EASE* SHOPPING LIST

Here is a very basic shopping list that includes many of the dry or shelf-stable items used in this book. Buy organic when possible. Some of these items should be refrigerated after purchase and *must* be refrigerated after opening.

For Your Pantry

- almonds; raw and roasted (refrigerate after opening)
- baking powder (aluminum-free variety)
- baking soda (aluminum-free variety)
- balsamic vinegar
- beans; black beans, white beans, kidney beans and garbanzo beans (chickpeas), canned (refrigerate after opening)
- bouillon cube, vegan, non-hydrogenated
- bread; whole-grain and sprouted varieties (refrigerate after purchase)
- brown rice; long- and short-grain and basmati
- brown sugar, Sucanat (or your preferred dry sweetener), vegan
- capers (refrigerate after opening)
- cashews; raw and roasted (refrigerate after purchase)
- catsup (refrigerate after opening)
- chocolate chips, dark vegan
- cocoa powder, unsweetened
- coconut, unsweetened; raw, shredded and flaked
- cornmeal; finely ground and polenta (refrigerate after purchase)
- cranberries, dried
- dark chocolate bar, vegan, sweetened (not baking variety)
- dates (Medjool preferred)
- Dijon mustard (refrigerate after opening)
- extra-virgin olive oil
- flaxseeds, golden (refrigerate after opening if pre-ground)
- maple syrup; Grades A dark amber or B (refrigerate after opening)
- marinara sauce, jarred, vegan (refrigerate after opening)
- molasses, unsulphured, blackstrap (refrigerate after opening)
- nondairy milk, aseptic container; sweetened, unsweetened and chocolate varieties such as almond, oat, cashew, rice, hazelnut, coconut and soy (refrigerate after opening)
- oats, rolled
- olives, jarred; green and Kalamata (refrigerate after opening)
- pasta, whole-grain or gluten-free; penne, fusilli, lasagna, macaroni, spaghetti, *conchiglie* and/or jumbo shell varieties
- peanut butter, non-hydrogenated (refrigerate after opening)

- pecans (refrigerate after purchase)
- powdered sugar, vegan
- preserves; apricot, blueberry, raspberry and strawberry (refrigerate after opening)
- pumpkin seeds, without hulls; raw or roasted (refrigerate after purchase)
- quinoa; red, white, black or mixed
- raisins
- salsa, jarred (refrigerate after opening)
- sunflower seeds; raw or roasted (refrigerate after purchase)
- tahini (refrigerate after opening)
- tamari; regular and/or reduced-sodium (refrigerate after opening)
- tomatoes, canned, jarred or aseptic container; whole peeled, diced and crushed varieties (refrigerate in glass container after opening)
- vanilla extract
- vegetable broth, canned or aseptic container (refrigerate after opening)
- walnuts; whole and chopped (refrigerate or freeze after purchase)
- wheat germ; raw or toasted (refrigerate after opening)

For Your Spice Cabinet

Cooking with dried herbs and spices is an easy way to add layers of appetizing flavors to your dishes. I love incorporating dried herbs and spices into my daily meals and snacks. One of my favorite ways to save time in the kitchen is to use pre-mixed seasonings like an all-purpose or Italian blend. For example, when I want to give my recipes an Italian accent, I grab just one jar of Italian seasoning blend and use that instead of opening six or seven jars of herbs (like basil, oregano, thyme, sage, rosemary and marjoram). It's *so* much easier and less time-consuming when you are in a hurry to get a mouthwatering meal on the table!

Here's a basic list of dried herbs, spices and seasoning blends to keep stocked in your spice cabinet.

- All-Purpose Seasoning Blend
- Basil
- Black Pepper, in grinder
- Cayenne Pepper
- Chili Powder
- Cinnamon
- Cumin
- Dill Weed
- Garam Masala
- Garlic Powder
- Italian Seasoning Blend
- Marjoram
- Pumpkin Pie Spice or Apple Pie Spice
- Oregano
- Paprika, regular and smoked
- Parsley
- Red Pepper Flakes, crushed
- Rosemary, crushed
- Sea salt and/or Himalayan Pink Salt
- Turmeric

Fruits and Veggies

Fresh fruits and vegetables make up the foundation of great plant-based cooking. Buy organic or certified naturally grown produce when it is available and/or economically feasible. Here's a short list of garden-fresh produce used in the recipes in this book:

- Apples
- Asparagus
- Avocado
- Bananas
- Bell peppers; orange, yellow, red, green
- Blueberries
- Broccoli
- Cabbage
- Carrots
- Cauliflower
- Celery
- Cucumber
- Eggplant
- Garlic, fresh
- Ginger, fresh
- Green beans

- Kale; curly, red or *lacinato* ("dinosaur kale")
- Lemon
- Lettuce; romaine, leafy green and red, spring green mix
- Mushrooms; cremini, white button, shiitake and portobello
- Onions; purple or red, sweet and yellow
- Potatoes; white, russet and red
- Scallions
- Spinach; regular and baby
- Squash; acorn, butternut, summer and zucchini
- Strawberries
- Sweet potatoes and/or yams
- Tomatoes, all varieties

Refrigerated and Frozen Items

Here are a few basic items that are found in the refrigerated or frozen section of the supermarket or health food store, making it easier to whip up tasty vegan meals in a flash:

- Cheese, vegan; shredded, melting variety in several flavors
- Cream cheese, vegan
- Frozen fruit; raspberries, blueberries, mangos and strawberries
- Seitan; cubes, crumbled and strips
- Tempeh; 3- and 5-grain varieties
- Tofu, regular and silken; soft, firm and extra-firm
- Tofu, baked and flavored
- Tortillas; whole-grain, flavored and gluten-free
- Whole wheat flour, regular and pastry (may be found in the baking aisle or refrigerated section of your supermarket; should be refrigerated after purchase)

NO-OIL COOKING

Many of us are watching our waistlines and improving our health by eliminating or lowering the amount of oil used in our daily recipes. But how do you eliminate oil from recipes while making them tasty, too?

When preparing savory dishes like stir-fries, casseroles and sauces, simply replace all of the oil called for in a recipe with vegetable broth or water. Use two or three tablespoons of broth or water to replace one tablespoon of oil, then add more broth or water (about two tablespoons at a time) as needed to keep the pan from getting dry.

When preparing sweet baked goods like pies, muffins, biscuits, quick breads or cakes, use fresh apple purée or mashed bananas to replace all of the oil and some of the sugar. Begin by adding the apple purée or mashed bananas in the same ratio you would add oil to the recipe. Then add more liquid (water or nondairy milk) to the batter, about 3 tablespoons at a time, until the desired consistency is achieved. Then decrease the sugar called for in the recipe by 25 to 50 percent, depending upon your individual taste. Once you try a few of the baked goods recipes in this book, you'll get the hang of it and enjoy experimenting on your own!

SALT AND PEPPER—PLEASE OR NO THANKS?

Why aren't exact amounts of salt and pepper included in some of the recipes in this book? If a recipe requires a precise amount of salt or pepper to make it taste optimal, the exact amount is included in the ingredients list. If the inclusion of either salt or pepper is only a matter of choice, I have left it up to you to season as desired.

Easy Eco-Clean Your Kitchen

H ere's a sage word of advice about keeping a "Vegan-*Ease-y*" clean kitchen. (*I could write a whole book just about this subject!*)

Think of it this way: You have just finished making your family a super healthy, vegan meal and now it's time to clean the kitchen. These days, there are many great nontoxic cleaning products that can be purchased at your local supermarket, health food store, or ordered online. I recommend you experiment with the wide selection you'll find and then choose the ones that work best for you and your family. Search for products that use renewable, nontoxic, phosphate-free, biodegradable ingredients that are not tested on animals. These cleaners are usually kinder to our planet, people and pets.

Simple baking soda is "eco-nomical" *and* eco-friendly and is one of my favorite all-purpose cleansers. Kept in a shaker, it's perfect for scrubbing sinks, countertops, even cleaning the oven. Baking soda outshines all other cleansers for safely removing stubborn food particles stuck to casserole dishes. To use, sprinkle some baking soda on the surface to be cleaned and let it set a few minutes. Scrub away the dirt with a moist sponge or cloth, then rinse well and thoroughly dry. Your pots and pans will really shine! Who knew cleaning could be so easy?

Table of Equivalent Measures

Here is a must-have list for any home cook. Use it for easily doubling or tripling recipes, adapting pre-existing recipes or cutting a recipe in half.

This . . .	Equals this . . .
3 teaspoons	1 tablespoon
4 tablespoons	¼ cup
8 tablespoons	½ cup
12 tablespoons	¾ cup
16 tablespoons	1 cup (or 8 ounces)
2 cups	1 pint (or 16 ounces)
4 cups	1 quart (or 32 ounces)
4 quarts	1 gallon (or 128 ounces)

Nutrition and the Plant-Based Diet

I am often asked about the nutritional basics of a plant-based diet. I strongly believe these types of queries are best answered by a registered dietitian, so I am honored that Julieanna Hever, *The Plant-Based Dietitian*, will share some words of wisdom with us here. For more comprehensive information about the nutritional benefits of eating vegan, Julieanna's book, *The Vegiterranean Diet*, makes for excellent supplemental reading to Vegan-*Ease*.

PLANT-BASED NUTRITION 101 *by Julieanna Hever, MS, RD, CPT*

Nutrient Know-How

One of the most commonly asked questions regarding a vegan diet is, "Where do you get your nutrients such as protein, vitamin B12, vitamin D or calcium?"

A well-planned plant-based diet consists of vegetables, fruits, whole grains, legumes, herbs and spices, with a small amount of nuts and seeds. Half of your plate (or diet) should consist of vegetables and fruits, which is in agreement with the Unites States Department of Agriculture, American Cancer Society and American Heart Association. Veggies (especially leafy greens) and fruits are the most nutrient-dense foods on the planet. They are chock-full of nutrients, antioxidants and phytochemicals, especially fiber, potassium, magnesium, iron, folate and vitamins C and A.

Legumes (beans, lentils, peas and soy foods) are also exquisitely nutritionally dense and are excellent sources of lysine, an amino acid that may otherwise fall short in a plant-based diet. They are loaded with fiber, calcium, iron, zinc and selenium. Aim to consume one to one-and-a-half cups of legumes each day.

Meals can be bulked up and diversified using whole grains such as buckwheat, oats, quinoa and brown rice. Grains are considered "whole" when they have their bran and germ intact, along with the endosperm. This ensures maintenance of the fiber and multiple other key nutrients.

Nuts are brimming with essential fats, protein, fiber, vitamin E and plant sterols, and have been shown to promote cardiovascular health and protect against type 2 diabetes, gallstones, macular degeneration and obesity. Research seems to consistently support including one to two ounces (30 to 60 grams) of nuts per day to achieve these health benefits. Seeds are also special because they have well-balanced essential fat ratios and contain several trace minerals and phytochemicals. Add one to two tablespoons per day to boost overall nutrition. Healthy sources of fats are found primarily in nuts, seeds, avocados and olives. For added flavor diversity and a bonus dose of phytochemicals, herbs and spices can be enjoyed as desired.

WHAT ABOUT PROTEIN?

Recommended protein intake[1] is based on your weight. Although it is quite popular for people to pursue protein in hefty doses, we only need approximately 10 percent of kcals to come from protein in order to meet our needs. (In fact, excessive protein can be harmful, taxing the kidneys, promoting gout and other chronic diseases, particularly when sourced from animal products). Protein is found abundantly throughout the plant world and the only way not to consume enough is to subsist on highly processed foods or to not eat adequate calories to meet your needs. Foods that are protein powerhouses include legumes, nuts and nut butters, seeds and seed butters, soy foods and intact whole grains.

HOW DO I GET VITAMIN B12?

Cobalamin, the technical name for vitamin B12, is the only nutrient not directly available from plants. Basically, if you don't eat animal products and are not supplementing, you are at a high risk for deficiency. Fortunately, however, this is easily remedied.

With a vegan diet, vitamin B12 can indeed be found in fortified plant milks, cereals, or nutritional yeast. Still, these may not be dependable sources of B12. Despite claims that fermented foods, spirulina, chlorella, certain mushrooms and sea vegetables can provide B12, they are not usually biologically active and can thereby promote deficiency. The most reliable, cost-effective and safe method of avoiding deficiency for vegans is to take a B12 supplement.

Because your body can only absorb approximately 1.5 to 2.0 micrograms at a time, supplement with a dose greater than the RDA to ensure adequate intake. A generally agreed-upon recommendation is 2,000 to 2,500 micrograms per week, which can be split into daily doses or into two to three doses of 1,000 micrograms each per week to help enhance absorption. Vitamin B12 is water soluble, so toxicity is rare.

WHERE DO I GET MY VITAMIN D?

Vitamin D, scientifically known as calciferol, is also considered the "sunshine vitamin." This is because it is the only nutrient that is obtained from exposure to the sun. Although vitamin D is treated as a vitamin, it is technically a prohormone because it is produced by your skin as the result of exposure to ultraviolet B (UVB) sun radiation and then converted into its active form by your liver and kidneys.

Ask your physician to check your blood levels of vitamin D at your next visit. If you turn out to be low, try sun therapy first: Find a way to be outside in the sunshine in the middle of peak hours (usually between 10 a.m. and 3 p.m.) for five to thirty minutes, at least twice per week. Do this with as much sunscreen-free skin exposed as possible, though keeping your face and eyes protected with sunscreen, sunglasses and/or a hat. Make sure your skin does not turn pink. This may take a few trials to find the right amount of time, so err on the side of less time to avoid sunburn until you find what is best for you.

There are many variables that can impact your absorption of UVB rays, including environmental issues such as cloud cover, smog, latitude, shade and glass, as well as physical factors, including skin color, age and fat. Thus, sun therapy is often not effective at bringing up blood D levels. If that is the case, you may consider supplementing. Ask your physician or dietitian for a recommended dose; because vitamin D is fat soluble, excess amounts are stored in fatty tissue. As a result, you do not want to take more than you need.

HOW CAN I GET ENOUGH CALCIUM?

Calcium is the most abundant mineral found in the human body. Calcium is one of many nutrients of concern with respect to bone health. Excellent plant sources of calcium include leafy green vegetables—especially bok choy, broccoli, napa cabbage, collard greens, dandelion greens, kale, turnip greens and watercress—as well as fortified plant milks, calcium-set tofu, dried figs, sesame seeds and tahini, tempeh, almonds and almond butter, oranges, sweet potatoes and beans.

Regardless of how much calcium you consume, what matters most is how much you actually absorb. There are certain key factors that impact calcium absorption, including:

- How much you consume. You can only absorb about 500 milligrams at a time and absorption decreases as calcium intake increases.

- Your age. Calcium absorption peaks in infants and children, as they are rapidly growing bone, and then progressively decreases as we age.

- Phytates, compounds found in whole grains, beans, seeds, nuts and wheat bran, can bind with calcium as well as with other minerals and inhibit absorption. Soaking, sprouting, leavening and fermenting improve absorption.

- Oxalates are elements found in some leafy green vegetables (such as spinach, Swiss chard, collard greens, parsley, leeks and beet greens), berries, almonds, cashews, peanuts, soybeans, okra, quinoa, cocoa, tea and chocolate. They may also somewhat inhibit absorption of calcium and other minerals, though some may still be absorbed. Aim for variety in the foods you eat on a day-to-day basis to improve overall absorption.

- Monitor your blood levels of vitamin D because you need them to be optimal to absorb calcium.

- Be careful of excessive intakes of sodium, protein, caffeine and phosphorus (as from sodas) because these nutrients may enhance calcium loss as well.

Here is a convenient chart highlighting excellent sources of notable nutrients:

Notable Nutrient Sources
The Plant-Based Dietitian
www.PlantBasedDietitian.com

Nutrient	Sources
Protein	legumes (beans, lentils, peas, peanuts), nuts, seeds, leafy green vegetables, (non-GMO) soy products
Omega-3 Fats	seeds (chia, hemp, flax), leafy green vegetables, microalgae, (non-GMO) soybeans and soy products, walnuts, wheat germ.
Fiber	vegetables, fruits (berries, pears, papaya, dried fruits), avocado, legumes (beans, lentils, peas), nuts, seeds, whole grains
Calcium	low oxalate leafy greens (broccoli, bok choy, cabbage, collard, dandelion, kale, watercress), calcium-set tofu, almonds, almond butter, fortified plant milks, sesame seeds, tahini, figs, blackstrap molasses
Iodine	sea vegetables (arame, dulse, nori, wakame), iodized salt
Iron	legumes (beans, lentils, peas), leafy greens, (non-GMO) soy products, quinoa, potatoes, dried fruit, dark chocolate, tahini, seeds (pumpkin, sesame, sunflower), sea vegetables (dulse, nori)
Zinc	legumes (beans, lentils, peas, peanuts), (non-GMO) soy products, nuts, seeds, oats
Choline	legumes (beans, peas, peanuts), bananas, broccoli, oats, oranges, quinoa, (non-GMO) soy products
Folate	leafy green vegetables, almonds, asparagus, avocado, beets, enriched grains (breads, pasta, rice), oranges, quinoa, nutritional yeast
Vitamin B12	fortified foods (nutritional yeast, plant milks), supplement (2,500 micrograms per week)
Vitamin C	fruits (especially berries, citrus, cantaloupe, kiwifruit, mango, papaya, pineapple), leafy green vegetables, potatoes, peas, bell peppers, chile peppers, tomatoes
Vitamin D	sun, fortified plant milks, supplement if deficient
Vitamin K	leafy green vegetables, sea vegetables, asparagus, avocado, broccoli, Brussels sprouts, cauliflower, lentils, peas, natto

Julieanna Hever, MS, RD, CPT   *Plant-Based Dietitian, Author, Host, Speaker, Health and Fitness Expert*

In conclusion, aim to follow a well-planned, plant-based diet consisting of vegetables, fruits, whole grains, legumes, herbs and spices, with a small amount of nuts and seeds, and be mindful to take a vitamin B12 supplement. Monitor your vitamin D levels in your blood and use sun therapy and/or supplement if you are low. Use the *Notable Nutrient Sources* chart to help ensure you are consuming all of the essential nutrients. To learn more about balancing wholesome plant foods for optimal, sustainable health, go to *www.plantbaseddietitian.com*.

Julieanna Hever, MS, RD, CPT

NOTE

[1] Institute of Medicine of the National Academies. "Dietary Reference Intakes: Macronutrients." Accessed on April 15, 2015.

PART II

the recipes

So easy, yet super tasty, these innovative appetizers are sure to impress. Using store-bought hummus makes it mega-quick, but for some extra pizzazz, try it with the *Lots of Garlic Hummus* (page 33).

Potato-Hummus Canapés

EASE FACTOR **1**   MAKES 6 SERVINGS

2 to 3 large baked and chilled russet or white potatoes

1 container (about 10 ounces) prepared hummus (or homemade hummus)

6 to 7 green queen olives with pimento, thinly sliced

1 teaspoon dried dill weed or 1 tablespoon chopped fresh dill

ut the cold, cooked potatoes into ¼-inch slices. Put each slice on a large serving platter and top with about 1 tablespoon of hummus. Top with an olive slice. Continue in this way with the remaining potato slices, arranging them in a pleasing manner on the platter as you go.

Lightly sprinkle the dill over the canapés and serve immediately.

 Chef's Note You may bake the potatoes up to two days before assembling this dish. Wrap them tightly and store in the refrigerator until using.

Amount per serving, based on 6 servings: 223 Calories; 5g Fat; 1g Saturated fat; 8g Protein; 191mg Sodium; 39g Total Carbohydrate; 2g Sugars; 6g Fiber

A simple, traditional dish, this combination satisfies as a perfect appetizer. Created by my friend Julieanna Hever, this delightful starter can be assembled in minutes to enjoy as a light snack in the afternoon or before dinner.

Julieanna's Easy Caprese

EASE FACTOR **1**   MAKES 2 TO 4 SERVINGS

2 large heirloom or beefsteak tomatoes, sliced into ½-inch thick slices

⅓ cup fresh basil leaves

4 ounces organic soft regular tofu, thinly sliced

2 to 3 tablespoons reduced balsamic vinegar

 ayer the tomato slices on a large plate. Evenly place the basil leaves over the tomatoes, followed by the tofu slices. Drizzle the vinegar over all. Serve immediately or store in an airtight container in the refrigerator for up to 2 days.

Julieanna's Note: You may use your favorite regular balsamic vinegar as is, or try reducing it. Pour at least triple the amount of vinegar called for in the recipe in a small saucepan. Bring the vinegar to a boil over medium heat, and then reduce the heat to low and simmer until at desired thickness, at least 20 to 30 minutes. Stored in an airtight container in the refrigerator, leftover reduced vinegar will keep for up to one week.

Recipe from The Vegiterranean Diet *reprinted with permission from Julieanna Hever and Da Capo Lifelong Books. Learn more about Julieanna on page 248.*

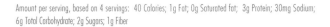

Amount per serving, based on 4 servings: 40 Calories; 1g Fat; 0g Saturated fat; 3g Protein; 30mg Sodium; 6g Total Carbohydrate; 2g Sugars; 1g Fiber

This quick hummus is ready in five minutes flat! Rich, smooth and full of garlicky flavor, it's accented with the tangy taste of freshly squeezed lemon juice and a tiny bit of heat from the chili powder.

Lots of Garlic Hummus

EASE FACTOR ①   MAKES 4 SERVINGS

1 cup chickpeas (garbanzo beans), drained and rinsed

¼ cup plus 2 tablespoons filtered or spring water, plus more as needed

5 cloves garlic, chopped

2 tablespoons sesame tahini

2 tablespoons freshly squeezed lemon juice

½ teaspoon chili powder, plus more for garnish

¼ teaspoon sea salt

ut all of the ingredients in a blender and process until smooth. Add a bit more water if needed to achieve desired consistency. Transfer the hummus to a pretty bowl and sprinkle the top with a pinch more chili powder, if desired, for a festive presentation.

Amount per serving, based on 4 servings: 115 Calories; 5g Fat; 1g Saturated fat; 5g Protein; 118mg Sodium; 13g Total Carbohydrate; 2g Sugars; 3g Fiber

Creamy, delicious and easy to make, this dip will impress your guests. Oh yeah—it's quick to make and good for you, too!

Ease-y White Bean Dip

EASE FACTOR ❶   MAKES 4 TO 6 SERVINGS

1 can (15 ounces) white beans, drained and rinsed

2 tablespoons filtered or spring water, plus more as needed

1 heaping tablespoon sesame tahini

1 tablespoon freshly squeezed lemon juice

1 large clove garlic, chopped

¼ teaspoon sea salt

Put all of the ingredients in a blender and process until smooth. Add a bit more water as needed to achieve desired consistency. Transfer to a pretty bowl and serve with Lively Lime Tortilla Chips (page 35), veggie sticks or whole-grain crackers.

Amount per serving, based on 6 servings: 101 Calories; 2g Fat; 0g Saturated fat; 6g Protein; 4mg Sodium; 16g Total Carbohydrate; 0g Sugars; 4g Fiber

This lively combination of spicy tortillas flavored with the zing of freshly squeezed lime juice and sea salt makes a healthy and refreshing change to oil-laden, prepackaged chips.

Lively Lime Tortilla Chips

EASE FACTOR   MAKES 4 SERVINGS

4 teaspoons freshly squeezed lime juice

4 whole-grain tortillas (spicy variety works best)

Coarse sea salt, to taste

Preheat the oven to 400 degrees F. Line two large, rimmed baking sheets with unbleached parchment paper. Pour the lime juice into a small bowl.

Put one tortilla on a large plate. Brush one side of the tortilla with a very thin layer of lime juice, using a pastry brush. Flip and repeat on the other side. Repeat with the remaining tortillas.

On a large cutting board, slice a lime-covered tortilla into chip-sized wedges or strips. Repeat with the remaining tortillas. Place the tortilla wedges in a single layer on the prepared baking sheets and sprinkle liberally with the coarse sea salt.

Bake for 10 to 20 minutes, or until the sides of the chips are crispy and slightly golden. Transfer the chips to a rack or large platter to cool. Serve warm or at room temperature.

Amount per serving, based on 4 servings: 110 Calories; 3g Fat; 2g Saturated fat; 3g Protein; 240mg Sodium; 19g Total Carbohydrate; 1 Sugars; 2g Fiber

Serving a snappy beverage with a sophisticated touch is simple with this refreshing recipe.

Sassy Seltzer with Raspberries

EASE FACTOR **1**   MAKES 4 TO 6 SERVINGS

16 to 24 large, fresh raspberries

1 bottle (25 to 33 ounces) lemon, lime or raspberry flavored seltzer or sparkling spring water, well chilled

Arrange 4 raspberries in the bottom of four to six champagne flutes. Slowly pour the flavored seltzer over top of the raspberries. Serve immediately.

Amount per serving, based on 6 servings: 11 Calories; 0g Fat; 0g Saturated fat; 0g Protein; 0mg Sodium; 2g Total Carbohydrate; 1g Sugars; 1g Fiber

I like to serve this refreshing summertime beverage to guests when they arrive for a casual afternoon party.

Berry Maple-Mint Iced Tea

EASE FACTOR ❶ | **MAKES 4 TO 6 SERVINGS**

5½ cups (room temperature) filtered or spring water

4 berry-flavored tea bags

2 heaping tablespoons maple syrup

4 to 6 fresh spearmint or peppermint sprigs

Ice cubes, for serving

Bring 4½ cups of the water to a boil over high heat in a teakettle or large pot. Put the tea bags in the bottom of a teapot. Pour the boiling water over the bags, cover and let steep for 1 hour. Remove the tea bags. Add the maple syrup and stir until blended.

Add the remaining 1 cup water and stir until blended. To serve, put plenty of ice into 4 to 6 large wine glasses or tall iced tea glasses. Pour the tea over the ice and tuck a sprig of mint into the cubes. Let stand 5 minutes so the mint flavor infuses into the tea. Serve immediately.

Amount per serving, based on 6 servings: 17 Calories; 0g Fat; 0g Saturated fat; 0g Protein; 1mg Sodium; 4g Total Carbohydrate; 4g Sugars; 0g Fiber

Two ingredients and five minutes of prep time produce a rich and creamy hot chocolate that rivals any I have tasted. The perfect treat to savor on a wintry afternoon!

Easy, Rich Hot Chocolate

EASE FACTOR ❶   MAKES 1 SERVING

1 cup plus 1 tablespoon nondairy milk

2 tablespoons vegan, dark chocolate chips

Put the nondairy milk and chocolate chips in a small saucepan. Bring to a simmer over medium-low heat and cook about 5 minutes, stirring frequently with a whisk, until the chips have melted. Pour into a coffee mug and let cool 5 minutes. Sip away!

Amount per serving, based on 1 serving: 221 Calories; 13g Fat; 6g Saturated fat; 10g Protein; 105mg Sodium; 19g Total Carbohydrate; 6g Sugars; 6g Fiber

This powerhouse blend of nutritious ingredients makes a healthful and delicious frosty treat any time of day.

Tropical Smoothie

EASE FACTOR

MAKES 2 TO 3 SERVINGS

2 tablespoons flaxseeds

2 frozen bananas (see note)

1 cup cubed pineapple, chilled

¾ cup baby spinach

1 cup coconut milk beverage, plus more as needed

¼ cup raw unsweetened shredded dried coconut

3 large Medjool dates, pitted

Put the flaxseeds in a high-performance blending appliance and process until very fine. Add the remaining ingredients and process until smooth and creamy. If the mixture is too thick, add more coconut milk beverage, ¼ cup at a time, to achieve the desired consistency, pulsing or blending briefly after each addition. Pour the mixture into pretty glasses. Serve immediately.

Chef's Note To freeze bananas, peel, then break each one into 3 or 4 pieces and put them in a resealable freezer bag. Seal and freeze for at least 12 hours or up to 1 week.

Amount per serving, based on 3 servings: 265 Calories; 7g Fat; 4g Saturated fat; 3g Protein; 80mg Sodium; 52g Total Carbohydrate; 37g Sugars; 7g Fiber

EASE-Y TWO-INGREDIENT RECIPE

Process chilled, cubed watermelon and lime juice in a blender, to make a refreshing summer drink.

Tofu, Sweet Pepper and Potato Scramble

EASE FACTOR ❷   **MAKES 2 TO 3 SERVINGS**

Sometimes we crave a low-fat breakfast dish that's satisfying too. This scramble totally fills the bill, with just the right texture and taste.

1 medium red onion, diced

⅓ cup plus 2 tablespoons filtered or spring water, plus more as needed

2 teaspoons reduced-sodium tamari

1 teaspoon olive oil

2 teaspoons Italian seasoning blend or all-purpose seasoning blend

2 medium russet potatoes, baked and cut in ½- to 1-inch cubes

⅛ teaspoon cayenne pepper

1 medium sweet red pepper, chopped

8 ounces extra-firm regular tofu, drained (see note)

½ teaspoon ground turmeric

Chef's Note If you prefer a soy-free scramble, use 1 cup cooked chickpeas (garbanzo beans), drained and rinsed in place of the tofu.

Put the onion, ⅓ cup water, 1 teaspoon tamari, olive oil and 1 teaspoon Italian seasoning in a large, nonstick skillet and cook for 5 minutes, stirring occasionally. Add the potatoes, 2 tablespoons water, 1 teaspoon Italian seasoning and the cayenne pepper. Cover and cook for 5 minutes, adding more water 2 tablespoons at a time as needed, if potatoes become dry.

Add the sweet pepper and 2 tablespoons water. Cover and cook for 5 minutes, adding more water 2 tablespoons at a time as needed, if potatoes become dry. Meanwhile, put the tofu, 1 teaspoon tamari and turmeric in a medium-sized bowl and mash using a potato masher or large fork until crumbly. Add the tofu mixture to the skillet, cover and cook, stirring occasionally, adding more water 1 tablespoon at a time, if tofu becomes dry. Uncover and cook 3 to 5 minutes until tofu becomes slightly golden. Serve immediately.

Amount per serving, based on 3 servings: 223 Calories; 5g Fat; 1g Saturated fat; 12g Protein; 33mg Sodium; 33g Total Carbohydrate; 4g Sugars; 5g Fiber

Spinach-Tomato Vegan Omelet

EASE FACTOR ③   MAKES 2 SERVINGS

I tried for years to create a tasty vegan omelet, so I was super excited when I came up with this oven-baked version. Because a tofu-based omelet is more delicate than the classic egg version, I have developed a jazzy method for helping it to stay together when serving. It takes a little bit of extra fuss, but is well worth the effort.

TOMATO LAYER

2 medium tomatoes, cut into ¼-inch thick slices

½ teaspoon dried thyme

¼ teaspoon sea salt

Several grinds of freshly ground pepper

SPINACH LAYER

5 to 6 cups *very* lightly packed baby spinach, washed and dried

TOFU "EGG" LAYER

1 block (14 to 16 ounces) firm regular tofu

½ teaspoon dried marjoram

¼ teaspoon ground turmeric

⅛ teaspoon smoked paprika

⅛ teaspoon cayenne pepper

ADDITIONAL INGREDIENTS

¼ teaspoon smoked paprika (for dusting top)

¼ cup shredded vegan cheese (optional)

Sea salt, to taste

Freshly ground pepper, to taste

Preheat the oven to 400 degrees F. Lightly coat with vegan margarine a heavy, ovenproof 10-inch round sauté pan or skillet with tight fitting lid.

Arrange the tomatoes in the prepared skillet by overlapping them slightly. Sprinkle the thyme, ¼ teaspoon salt and several grinds of black pepper evenly over the top of the tomatoes.

Top the tomato layer with all of the baby spinach, pressing it down slightly.

Put all of the tofu "egg" layer ingredients in a blender and process until smooth. Spread the tofu mixture evenly over the spinach, smoothing the top as you go.

Dust the top of the tofu layer with the additional ¼ teaspoon smoked paprika. Cover tightly and bake for 45 minutes. Put the pan on a wire rack and let cool for 5 minutes.

Carefully cut the omelet into two servings, by slicing down the middle. Gently lift one-half of the omelet out of the pan, using two very large, flat spatulas. Place it tomato side down onto a rimmed dinner plate. Place a second rimmed dinner plate of the same size *firmly* over top of the omelet and quickly flip it over to invert the omelet so the tomatoes will now be facing upward. Sprinkle the tomatoes with 2 tablespoons of the vegan cheese, if desired. Then, use the spatula to gently fold the omelet over. Proceed plating up the second half of the omelet in the same manner.

Spoon the sauce that remains in the bottom of the pan over each omelet. Season with sea salt and freshly ground pepper, to taste. Serve warm.

Amount per serving, based on 2 servings:
188 Calories; 11g Fat; 2g Saturated fat; 21g Protein; 107mg Sodium; 7g Total Carbohydrate; 2g Sugars; 4g Fiber

Nutritional Information with optional vegan cheese: Amount per serving, based on 2 servings: 234 Calories; 14g Fat; 3g Saturated fat; 22g Protein; 232mg Sodium; 11g Total Carbohydrate; 2g Sugars; 5g Fiber

Spinach-Tomato Vegan Omelet *(page 47), above*

Tofu Veg-Muffins, *below*

Tasty and hearty vegan baked goods are a crowd pleaser at breakfast, lunch, brunch or dinner.

muffins, quick breads and baked delights

6

Facing page: Lime and Coconut Corn Muffins, page 59

Tart and sweet flavors together make for a perfectly balanced, delicious muffin that you'll want to have on hand for all occasions!

Lemony Cornmeal and Cranberry Muffins

EASE FACTOR ❷   **MAKES 12 MUFFINS**

1 cup nondairy milk

¼ cup freshly squeezed lemon juice (about 2 medium lemons; zest the lemons first, before squeezing)

¼ cup maple syrup

4 tablespoons golden flaxseeds

1½ cups whole wheat flour

¾ cup fine grind corn meal

1 teaspoon baking powder

1 teaspoon baking soda

¼ teaspoon sea salt

½ cup Sucanat or brown sugar

1 heaping teaspoon lemon zest

1⅓ cup dried cranberries

Preheat the oven to 375 degrees F. Line a twelve-cup standard muffin pan with paper liners.

Put the nondairy milk, lemon juice and maple syrup in a small bowl and stir to combine. Let stand for 5 minutes to make vegan "buttermilk."

Put the flaxseeds in a high-performance blending appliance and process into fine flour. Put the flaxseed flour into a large bowl. Add the whole wheat flour, corn meal, baking powder, baking soda and salt, stirring with a dry whisk to combine. Add the Sucanat (or brown sugar) and lemon zest; stir to combine.

Stir in the vegan "buttermilk" to make a batter. Add the cranberries and mix just until incorporated.

Mound the batter into the prepared muffin cups. Bake for 28 to 30 minutes, or until slightly golden and a toothpick inserted in the center of a muffin comes out clean. Put the pan on a wire rack. Let cool for 5 to 10 minutes. Remove the muffins. Serve warm or at room temperature. Covered tightly and stored in the refrigerator, leftover muffins will keep for about 3 days.

Amount per serving, based on 12 servings: 184 Calories; 2g Fat; 0g Saturated fat; 4g Protein; 11mg Sodium; 41g Total Carbohydrate; 21g Sugars; 4g Fiber

Truly easy and quick to prepare, these moist and sweet, low-fat beauties make a great "grab and go" breakfast treat or lunch box snack. Bonus: They're "eco-nomical" too!

Ease-y Raspberry-Lemon Muffins

EASE FACTOR ❶   **MAKES 12 MUFFINS**

2 cups plus 2 tablespoons whole wheat flour

1½ teaspoons baking soda

1 cup filtered or spring water

⅓ cup plus 1 tablespoon maple syrup

⅓ cup freshly squeezed lemon juice

12 heaping teaspoons raspberry preserves (see note)

 reheat the oven to 375 degrees F. Line a twelve-cup standard muffin pan with paper liners.

Put the whole wheat flour and baking soda in a large bowl and stir with a dry whisk to combine. Stir in the water, ⅓ maple syrup and lemon juice; mix just until incorporated.

Fill each prepared muffin cup one-half full with the batter. Make a small well in the center with a spoon or your finger. Spoon 1 heaping teaspoon of the preserves into the well. Top with the remaining batter, distributing it evenly among the muffin cups. Smooth out the top of each muffin with a rubber spatula. Bake for 20 to 24 minutes, or until golden and a toothpick inserted in the side of a muffin comes out clean. Put the pan on a wire rack and let cool for 3 minutes.

Meanwhile, pour 1 tablespoon of maple syrup in a small bowl. Carefully remove the muffins from the pan and transfer them to a wire rack. Glaze the top of each muffin with a bit of maple syrup while it is still hot, using a pastry brush or back of a small spoon. Let the muffins cool for 25 to 30 minutes. Gently peel off the paper liners. Serve warm.

Covered tightly and stored in the refrigerator, leftover muffins will keep for about 2 days.

 Chef's Note You may use your preferred flavor of preserves, jelly or jam in this recipe.

Amount per serving, based on 12 servings: 155 Calories; 1g Fat; 0g Saturated fat; 3g Protein; 8mg Sodium; 36g Total Carbohydrate; 16g Sugars; 2g Fiber

These bountiful beauties make a tempting breakfast treat, lunchbox item or after-school snack. Isn't it nice when something so tasty happens to be filled with nutritious ingredients?

Bountiful Blueberry Bars

EASE FACTOR **2**   MAKES 10 BARS

4 tablespoons golden flaxseeds

2 large ripe bananas

¼ cup Sucanat or brown sugar

2 heaping tablespoons blueberry preserves

1 teaspoon vanilla extract

2 cups rolled oats

¼ cup raw unsweetened shredded dried coconut

1 cup fresh blueberries

Preheat the oven to 375 degrees F. Line an 8-inch square baking pan with unbleached parchment paper, leaving 3- to 4-inch "wings" on two opposite sides of the pan.

Put the flaxseeds in a high-performance blending appliance and process into very fine flour. Put the bananas, Sucanat (or brown sugar), blueberry preserves and vanilla in a medium-sized bowl and mash with a potato masher or large fork into a chunky purée. Add the ground flaxseeds, oats and coconut; stir to combine. Gently fold in the fresh blueberries.

Spread the dough in an even layer in the prepared pan. Score into 10 bars using a table knife. Bake for 30 to 35 minutes, or until slightly golden around the edges. Put the pan on a heatproof surface. Using the parchment paper "wings" as handles, carefully lift the bars out of the pan in one piece. Transfer to a wire rack and let cool for 15 to 20 minutes.

Again, using the parchment paper "wings" as handles, transfer the bars to a cutting board and cut into 10 individual bars. Stored in an airtight container in the refrigerator, the bars will keep for 2 days.

Amount per serving, based on 10 servings: 145 Calories; 3g Fat; 1g Saturated fat; 3g Protein; 6mg Sodium; 29g Total Carbohydrate; 12g Sugars; 4g Fiber

This bread is a true quick bread in that it prepares for the oven in about 10 minutes. It's great slathered with whole fruit preserves or your favorite nut butter.

Banana Bread with Sunflower Seeds

EASE FACTOR 2

MAKES 1 LOAF

1⅓ cups sliced bananas (about 1 very large or 2 small)

1⅔ cups nondairy milk (a thicker variety works best)

2 cups whole wheat pastry flour

4 tablespoons ground golden flaxseeds

2¼ teaspoons baking powder

1 teaspoon ground cinnamon

¼ teaspoon sea salt

1 cup raw unsweetened shredded dried coconut

½ cup Sucanat or brown sugar

½ cup pitted and diced dates

½ cup roasted, unsalted sunflower seeds

Preheat the oven to 350 degrees F. Lightly coat a 9 x 5-inch loaf pan with vegan margarine.

Put the banana slices and ⅓ cup of the nondairy milk in a small bowl and mash until smooth using a potato masher or large fork.

Put the flour, flaxseeds, baking powder, cinnamon and sea salt in a large bowl and stir with a dry whisk to combine. Add the coconut and Sucanat (or brown sugar); stir with the whisk to combine. Stir in the remaining 1⅓ cups of nondairy milk and mix until incorporated. Fold in the dates and sunflower seeds. Transfer the mixture to the prepared pan and smooth the top. Bake for 45 to 55 minutes, or until a toothpick inserted in the center of the bread comes out clean. Put the pan on a wire rack and let cool 5 minutes. Loosen the sides of the bread with a knife. Carefully invert the loaf onto a wire rack. Let cool for 20 to 30 minutes before slicing. Covered tightly and stored in the refrigerator, the loaf will keep for 3 days.

Amount per serving, based on 1 loaf (12 slices): 258 Calories; 10g Fat; 6g Saturated fat; 6g Protein; 22mg Sodium; 39g Total Carbohydrate; 16g Sugars; 6g Fiber

This versatile quick bread is excellent served with jam; it also slices beautifully for sandwiches. It has a nice soft texture and, in a pinch, can take the place of a conventional loaf of yeast-based bread. Any way you slice it, it takes only twenty minutes to prepare for the oven.

Walnut-Orange Quick Bread

EASE FACTOR 3

MAKES 6 TO 8 SERVINGS

1¼ cups plus 2 tablespoons nondairy milk

3 tablespoons freshly squeezed orange juice (from 1 medium orange; zest the orange first, before squeezing)

4 tablespoons golden flaxseeds

2 cups whole wheat flour

3 tablespoons fine grind cornmeal

1 tablespoon toasted wheat germ

1 tablespoon baking powder

½ teaspoon ground cinnamon

1 teaspoon orange zest

½ cup lightly packed brown sugar

½ cup plus 1 tablespoon rolled oats

½ cup chopped walnuts

1 cup sliced ripe banana

2 tablespoons filtered or spring water

1 teaspoon extra-virgin olive oil, plus more for coating pan

Preheat the oven to 375 degrees F. Lightly oil a 9 x 5-inch loaf pan. Line the width of the interior of the pan with unbleached parchment paper, allowing a 2- to 3-inch overhang on each side of the pan. This will allow you to easily lift the loaf out of the pan, once it is baked.

Put the nondairy milk and orange juice in a small bowl and stir to combine. Let the mixture stand while preparing the rest of the ingredients.

Put the flaxseeds in a high-performance blending appliance and process into fine flour. Transfer the flaxseed flour to a large bowl. Add the whole wheat flour, cornmeal, wheat germ, baking powder and cinnamon to the flaxseed flour; stir with a dry whisk to combine (see note).

Finely mince the orange zest. Add the brown sugar and orange zest to the flaxseed flour mixture; stir to combine. Stir in ½ cup of rolled oats and the walnuts.

Put the banana, water and olive oil in a blender and process until smooth.

Add the banana mixture and the nondairy milk/ orange juice combination to the dry ingredients and stir just until incorporated. Mound the batter into the prepared loaf pan and smooth out the top using a rubber spatula. Sprinkle 1 tablespoon of rolled oats evenly over the top of the loaf.

Amount per serving, based on 8 servings: 288 Calories; 8g Fat; 1g Saturated fat; 8g Protein; 18mg Sodium; 49g Total Carbohydrate; 17g Sugars; 6g Fiber

Bake for 50 minutes, or until a toothpick inserted in the middle of the bread comes out clean. Put the pan on a wire rack. Using the parchment paper "wings" as handles, gently lift the bread from the pan and place it on the wire rack. Carefully peel off the parchment paper. Let the bread cool for 30 minutes before slicing.

Wrapped tightly and stored in the refrigerator, leftover bread will keep for about 3 days.

Chef's Note If you like a salty flavor in your bread, you may add ¼ teaspoon of salt before whisking together the dry ingredients.

Hot soups stand front and center as a main dish in colder seasons, while refreshing, chilled soups are perfect as sizzling summer fare.

simple soups

7

Facing page: Roasted Cauliflower and Green Pea Soup, page 76

Butternut Squash Soup with Quick Cashew "Cream"

EASE FACTOR 2   MAKES 4 TO 6 SERVINGS

This simple-to-prepare potage is rich in taste and creamy in texture, without the use of dairy. A quick cashew "cream" (no pre-soaking of the cashews required) adds a touch of elegance, and the coconut milk beverage adds richness and depth to this impressive soup.

5½ cups cubed butternut squash, (about 1 medium squash, peeled, seeded and cut in 1½-inch pieces)

1 tablespoon extra-virgin olive oil

1 tablespoon Italian seasoning blend

¼ teaspoon sea salt

⅔ cup raw cashews

2½ cups filtered or spring water, plus more as needed

½ cup unsweetened coconut milk beverage or nondairy milk of your choice

4 to 6 basil leaves, for garnish (optional)

Preheat the oven to 400 degrees F. Line a large, rimmed baking sheet with unbleached parchment paper.

Put the cubed squash, olive oil and Italian seasoning in a large bowl and toss gently until thoroughly coated. Arrange the squash in a single layer on the prepared pan. Bake for 50 minutes, stirring once or twice, until the squash is soft and slightly golden. Put the pan on a wire rack and sprinkle with the sea salt. Let the squash cool for 25 to 30 minutes (see note).

Meanwhile, put the cashews and ½ cup water in a high-performance blending appliance and process until smooth and creamy. Transfer the cashew "cream" to a small bowl, leaving about 2 heaping

Rich Black Bean Soup

EASE FACTOR **2**   MAKES 4 SERVINGS

This surprisingly flavorful and hearty soup uses canned black beans, veggies and a few other ready pantry items to make it quite possibly the easiest supper of the week! Extra hungry? Try serving it with Smoky Tempeh Sticks (page 53) on the side.

1 large onion, chopped

1 teaspoon chili powder

¼ teaspoon ground turmeric

¼ teaspoon ground cumin

1 cup plus 3 tablespoons filtered or spring water, plus more as needed

1⅓ cups peeled and diced sweet potatoes

2 cups diced tomatoes

1 teaspoon reduced-sodium tamari or ½ teaspoon sea salt

1 can (15 ounces) black beans, drained, rinsed and lightly mashed

¼ teaspoon dried cilantro or 1 teaspoon chopped fresh cilantro

Scant ⅛ teaspoon cayenne pepper

Put the onion, chili powder, turmeric, cumin and 3 tablespoons water in a large soup pot. Cook over medium heat for 2 minutes. Add the sweet potatoes, cover and cook, stirring occasionally, for 7 minutes, adding more water, 2 tablespoons at a time, as needed to prevent sticking.

Meanwhile, put the tomatoes and tamari or salt in a medium-sized bowl and lightly mash using a potato masher or the back of a large wooden spoon. Add the tomato mixture to the pot, cover and cook 5 minutes. Stir in the black beans, 1 cup water, cilantro and cayenne. Cover and cook for 12 to 15 minutes, or until the sweet potatoes are soft and the beans are heated through, adding more water as needed, if the soup seems too thick. Serve piping hot with a crisp green salad and crusty whole-grain bread on the side.

Amount per serving, based on 4 servings: 178 Calories; 0g Fat; 0g Saturated fat; 8g Protein; 375mg Sodium; 37g Total Carbohydrate; 9g Sugars; 9g Fiber

Whether first course or main course, based in greens or grains, tossed with a sweet or savory dressing—a colorful salad always makes a meal shine.

speedy salads, dressings and sandwiches

Facing page: Vegan "Lox" and Bagel, page 100

Here's a festive and fabulous way to serve a first course salad, any time of the year. Spooned into tiny parfait or champagne glasses, this tasty combo provides a refreshing change to a standard green salad.

Avocado Salad Parfaits

EASE FACTOR **1**   MAKES 4 TO 5 SERVINGS

DRESSING

Juice from half a medium lemon

1 small clove garlic, minced

1 teaspoon extra-virgin olive oil (see note)

⅛ teaspoon sea salt, plus more as needed

SALAD

10 to 14 grape or cherry tomatoes, halved or quartered

1 medium-to-large avocado, pit removed, peeled and diced

 ut all of the dressing ingredients in a small bowl and whisk briskly to emulsify. Put all of the salad ingredients in a medium-sized bowl. Pour in the dressing and gently stir to combine. Season with more salt, to taste. Cover and refrigerate 30 to 60 minutes before serving. To serve as a fancy first course, spoon into pretty glasses, displayed on a decorative plate.

Chef's Note For an oil-free dressing, omit the olive oil and proceed with the recipe as directed.

Amount per serving, based on 5 servings: 54 Calories; 4g Fat; 1g Saturated fat; 1g Protein; 4mg Sodium; 5g Total Carbohydrate; 1g Sugars; 2g Fiber

These tempting taco bowls make the perfect hearty lunch or light supper. Quick to make, these crisp, baked tortillas serve as the base, while the creamy, flavorful avocado and leafy green filling creates a true "one-dish" meal or generous first-course appetizer. Great for company, too!

Guacamole Taco Salad Bowls

EASE FACTOR 3   **MAKES 4 SERVINGS**

TACO BOWLS

4 8- to 10-inch whole-grain tortillas (spicy variety works well)

SALAD

2 large ripe avocados

2 tablespoons freshly squeezed lemon juice

1 teaspoon chili powder

¼ teaspoon ground turmeric

¼ teaspoon smoked paprika

¼ teaspoon sea salt, plus more as needed

1/16 to ⅛ teaspoon cayenne pepper (optional)

1 medium tomato, diced

½ medium sweet onion, diced

2½ cups thinly sliced romaine lettuce

¼ cup chopped fresh parsley or cilantro, for garnish (optional)

Zest of one lemon, for garnish (optional)

Preheat the oven to 400 degrees F. Line a medium, rimmed baking pan with unbleached parchment paper.

Arrange four small oven-safe bowls upside down on the prepared pan. Drape a tortilla over the bottom of each bowl, arranging it in the shape of an upside-down "bowl." Bake for 10 to 15 minutes, or until the tortillas are crisp and almost firm to the touch, checking them often so they do not burn. *Carefully* transfer the pan with the bowls on it to a wire rack and let cool at least 5 minutes before serving (see note).

Meanwhile, to prepare the guacamole, peel, pit, and rough chop the avocados. Put the chopped avocados, lemon juice, chili powder, turmeric, smoked paprika, sea salt and cayenne pepper (optional) in a medium-sized bowl and mash with a potato masher or large fork until combined. Gently fold in the tomatoes and onion.

To assemble the salads, carefully remove each cooled taco "bowl" and place it in the center of a medium-sized salad plate. Place one-quarter of the sliced romaine in the bottom of each taco "bowl." Top with one-quarter of the guacamole mixture. Garnish with a sprinkle of chopped fresh parsley or cilantro, and lemon zest (optional). Serve immediately.

Chef's Note Taco bowls may be prepared up to 6 hours before serving. After cooling, keep loosely covered until you are ready to assemble the salads.

Amount per serving, based on 4 servings: 229 Calories; 14g Fat; 3g Saturated fat; 5g Protein; 253mg Sodium; 27g Total Carbohydrate; 6g Sugars; 7g Fiber

Mini Taco Bowls: Start with 2 tortillas. Cut each tortilla into three circles, using a 4- to 5-inch round cookie
cutter. Invert a six-cup standard muffin pan on a medium-sized, rimmed baking sheet. Drape each tortilla
round over the bottom of a muffin cup, pressing it gently into a mini "bowl" shape. Put another muffin pan
of the same size directly over the tortillas and press
gently to hold the tortillas in place while baking.

Bake in a preheated 400 degree F. oven for 8 minutes. Carefully remove the top muffin pan and bake
for 6 to 10 minutes more, or until the tortillas are
crisp and almost set, checking them often.

Transfer to a wire rack and let cool at least 5 minutes before filling with some of the guacamole filling
(mini bowls will need only half of the salad filling indi-
cated in the recipe). Or fill with your preferred hummus
or salsa. Wonderful for an appetizer or first course.

This tantalizing summertime salad is one that I like to serve when I'm entertaining. Marinating the tofu in this lively combination of Greek-style herbs and spices makes a delightful vegan "cheese." Even if you are not a fan of tofu, you'll appreciate this tasty twist on a classic salad.

Chickpea-Tomato Salad with Tofu "Feta"

EASE FACTOR ❸   MAKES 4 SERVINGS

GREEK-STYLE VEGAN "FETA"

8 ounces firm or extra-firm regular tofu, well-drained

1 tablespoon freshly squeezed lemon juice

1 tablespoon plus 1 teaspoon extra-virgin olive oil

1 teaspoon Italian seasoning blend

¼ teaspoon garlic powder

¼ teaspoon sea salt, plus more as needed

CHICKPEA SALAD

1 can (15 ounces) chickpeas (garbanzo beans), drained and rinsed

1 medium cucumber, peeled, seeded and cubed

1 cup diced sweet red bell pepper

½ pint grape or cherry tomatoes, halved

½ cup diced onion

2 tablespoons capers, drained and rinsed

2 tablespoons chopped fresh parsley

1 teaspoon Italian seasoning blend

¼ teaspoon sea salt, plus more as needed

Freshly ground black pepper, to taste

Amount per serving, based on 4 servings: 288 Calories; 14g Fat; 2g Saturated fat; 11g Protein; 330mg Sodium; 32g Total Carbohydrate; 5g Sugars; 7g Fiber

T o make the "feta," put the tofu in a medium-sized bowl. Using your fingers or a fork, crumble the tofu until it resembles the texture of feta cheese. Add the lemon juice, oil, Italian seasoning, garlic powder and salt. Gently stir to combine. Cover and refrigerate a minimum of 2 hours or up to 12 hours.

To make the salad, put the chickpeas, cucumber, red pepper, tomatoes, onion, capers, parsley, Italian seasoning and sea salt in a large bowl. Gen-

I was inspired by the herbs from my deck garden as well as some beautiful grape tomatoes at my local farm market to create this refreshing summer salad.

Grape Tomato, Avocado and Fresh Herb Salad

EASE FACTOR ①   **MAKES 2 TO 4 SERVINGS**

DRESSING

2 tablespoons freshly squeezed lemon juice

1 tablespoon extra-virgin olive oil

1 clove garlic, minced

⅛ teaspoon sea salt, plus more to taste

Several grinds of freshly ground pepper, plus more to taste

SALAD

1 cup cooked and chilled black beans (see note)

8 ounces grape tomatoes, halved

2 medium avocados, pitted, peeled and cubed

¼ cup lightly packed, chopped fresh basil

2 tablespoons chopped fresh parsley

ut the dressing ingredients in a small bowl and whisk briskly to emulsify. Put all of the salad ingredients in a medium-sized bowl, pour in the dressing and toss gently to combine. Let stand 15 minutes to marry the flavors. Season with salt and pepper, to taste, and serve.

> **Chef's Note** To save preparation time, you may use 1 cup canned black beans, drained and rinsed, if desired.

Amount per serving, based on 4 servings: 131 Calories; 6g Fat; 1g Saturated fat; 4g Protein; 113mg Sodium; 16g Total Carbohydrate; 2g Sugars; 6g Fiber

White beans and walnuts provide both a creamy texture and an excellent source of protein in this super-easy salad dressing, perfect to serve over leafy greens.

White Bean Dressing

EASE FACTOR   MAKES 4 TO 6 SERVINGS

1 can (15 ounces) white beans (cannellini work best), drained and rinsed

½ cup filtered or spring water, plus more as needed

⅓ cup chopped walnuts

2 small cloves garlic, chopped

1 tablespoon freshly squeezed lemon juice

¼ teaspoon dried basil

⅛ teaspoon sea salt, plus more as needed

Put all of the ingredients in a blender and process until creamy and smooth. Add more water, as needed, to achieve the desired consistency.

Amount per serving, based on 6 servings: 89 Calories; 4g Fat; 0g Saturated fat; 4g Protein; 227mg Sodium; 11g Total Carbohydrate; 0g Sugars; 5g Fiber

Two minutes is all you need to whisk together this tasty dressing. Easy to double or triple for a big batch, this quick recipe may become a staple to dress up your daily salads.

Three-Ingredient Dressing

EASE FACTOR   MAKES 2 SERVINGS

1 tablespoon freshly squeezed lemon juice

1 tablespoon extra-virgin olive oil

½ teaspoon maple syrup

ut the oil, lemon juice and maple syrup in a small mixing bowl and briskly whisk to emulsify.

Amount per serving, based on 2 servings: 64 Calories; 7g Fat; 1g Saturated fat; 0g Protein; 0mg Sodium; 1g Total Carbohydrate; 1g Sugars; 0g Fiber

From spaghetti to pizza, easy-to-prepare pasta dishes made with healthful wholesome ingredients are the world's favorite "fast food."

pastas and pizzas, pronto!

9

Facing page: White Lasagna with Mushrooms and Green Peas, page 118

Quickest. Spaghetti Sauce. Ever.

EASE FACTOR ❶ MAKES 4 SERVINGS

OK—three ingredients combined with fifteen minutes on the stovetop and you have a hearty and tasty sauce that is totally guest-worthy! Serve over your favorite whole-grain pasta and enjoy the compliments.

1 package (8 ounces) crumbled or ground seitan

1 jar (24 to 28 ounces) low-fat, vegan marinara sauce

10 to 14 large fresh basil leaves, torn in pieces

Put the seitan and marinara sauce in a large skillet. Cover and bring to a simmer over medium heat. Decrease the heat to medium-low, cover and cook for 10 to 15 minutes, stirring occasionally, until heated through. Add the basil. Cover and cook one minute more.

Serve over whole-grain spaghetti, capellini, penne or any other favorite style of pasta. You can also use this as a sauce in lasagna or a casserole.

Amount per serving, based on 4 servings: 174 Calories; 3g Fat; 0g Saturated fat; 15g Protein; 769mg Sodium; 22g Total Carbohydrate; 0g Sugars; 0g Fiber

VEGAN-*EASE-Y* TIP

I live in New Jersey and fresh tomatoes are only available a few months per year. For this reason, jarred, organic marinara sauce and salsa are both star staples in my pantry to keep on hand for making quick casseroles, pasta dishes, sauces and so much more.

Fusilli with Caper and Garlic Marinara Sauce

EASE FACTOR ❶

A handful of pantry items gets this sauce going on the stovetop in under five minutes! Just thirty minutes gets this zesty pasta dish onto your plate.

1 can (28 ounces) whole tomatoes, with juice

1 teaspoon reduced-sodium tamari or ½ teaspoon sea salt

3 cloves garlic, minced

1 teaspoon Italian seasoning blend

1 teaspoon dried basil or 1 table-spoon chopped fresh basil

¼ teaspoon crushed red pepper

2 tablespoons capers, drained and rinsed

¼ teaspoon sea salt (optional)

1 pound whole-grain fusilli or other pasta

ut the tomatoes, tamari (or salt), garlic, Italian seasoning, basil and crushed red pepper in a large skillet. Mash with a potato masher or back of a large spoon until the tomatoes are broken up into chunks. Cover and bring to a simmer over medium heat. Decrease the heat to medium-low and cook, stirring occasionally, for 25 minutes. Add the capers and cook for 5 minutes, or until the capers are heated through.

Meanwhile, bring a large pot of water to a boil over medium-high heat. Add ¼ teaspoon sea salt (optional). Stir in the fusilli. Decrease the heat to medium-low and cook, stirring occasionally, until tender but firm. Drain the fusilli and, while it's still piping hot, pour it over the tomato sauce in the large skillet. Toss gently until the fusilli and sauce are thoroughly combined. Serve immediately.

Amount per serving, based on 5 servings: 350 Calories; 3g Fat; 0g Saturated fat; 12g Protein; 351mg Sodium; 66g Total Carbohydrate; 8g Sugars; 8g Fiber

Laura's Spaghetti

EASE FACTOR ❸

When I crave a homemade spaghetti dinner, this is my "go-to" sauce. Chopped mushrooms make a great substitute for the ground meat, reminiscent of my Grandma's version. My mom makes a yummy version of this spaghetti sauce too; she includes diced green pepper, which adds a tasty touch.

1 large red or sweet onion, chopped

½ small bunch celery, with leaves, chopped

¼ cup filtered or spring water, plus more as needed

2 teaspoons reduced-sodium tamari

1 teaspoon Italian seasoning blend

¼ teaspoon crushed red pepper

8 ounces cremini mushrooms, chopped

2 cloves garlic, chopped

1 jar (24 to 28 ounces) low-fat vegan marinara sauce

8 to 10 large fresh basil leaves, torn in pieces

¼ teaspoon sea salt (optional)

1 pound whole-grain spaghetti or other pasta

ut the onion, celery, ¼ cup water, tamari, Italian seasoning and crushed red pepper in a large skillet. Cover and cook over medium heat, stirring occasionally, for 8 to 10 minutes. Add more water, 2 tablespoons at a time, if the mixture gets dry. Add the mushrooms, cover and cook, stirring occasionally, for 5 to 7 minutes, adding more water, if needed. Add the garlic, cover and cook for 2 minutes.

Decrease the heat to medium-low. Pour in the marinara sauce, cover and cook for 10 minutes (see note). Stir in the basil leaves, cover and cook 5 minutes more.

Meanwhile, bring a large pot of water to a boil over medium-high heat. Add ¼ teaspoon sea salt (optional). Stir in the spaghetti. Decrease the heat to medium-low and cook, stirring occasionally, until tender but firm. Drain the spaghetti.

To serve family-style, arrange the cooked spaghetti on a large platter and top with the sauce. For individual servings, divide the spaghetti into six to eight pasta bowls, spooning sauce over each portion. Serve immediately.

> **Chef's Note** This sauce can be prepared and then kept on a low-heat simmer for up to 45 minutes ahead of mealtime for your convenience.

Amount per serving, based on 8 servings: 271 Calories; 3g Fat; 0g Saturated fat; 10g Protein; 404mg Sodium; 53g Total Carbohydrate; 3g Sugars; 6g Fiber

Pasta *Prima-Very* Jazzy

EASE FACTOR ❸ | MAKES 4 SERVINGS

"Pasta Primavera" is full of vegetables and so is my Pasta *Prima-Very* Jazzy! Delectable oven-roasted veggies make this hearty dish totally *jazzylicious*. There *are* quite a few ingredients, but because the vegetables are roasted in the oven, you can still go about hosting your party, while the recipe prepares itself...well, almost!

4½ cups bite-sized broccoli florets

2½ cups chopped sweet onion

2 cups julienned carrots (thickly sliced)

2 tablespoons extra-virgin olive oil, plus more as needed

2 teaspoons garlic powder

2 teaspoons reduced-sodium tamari

4 medium tomatoes, chopped

½ teaspoon sea salt, plus more as needed

⅓ cup chopped fresh basil

2 teaspoons minced fresh garlic

1 teaspoon chopped fresh oregano

½ teaspoon chopped fresh thyme

¾ pound whole-grain pasta, such as penne, fusilli or spaghetti

Freshly ground black pepper, to taste

Preheat the oven to 425 degrees F. Line two large, rimmed baking sheets with unbleached parchment paper.

Put the broccoli florets, onion, carrots, 1 tablespoon olive oil, garlic powder and reduced-sodium tamari in a large bowl and toss to evenly coat. Spread the broccoli mixture in an even layer on one of the lined baking sheets. Spread the tomatoes in an even layer on the remaining lined baking sheet. Sprinkle the tomatoes with ¼ teaspoon sea salt.

Put the broccoli mixture on the center rack of the oven and put the tomatoes on the top rack (or on the rack that is farthest from your heating element). Bake for 15 to 25 minutes, or until the vegetables are roasted, *al dente*.

Put 1 tablespoon of olive oil, basil, garlic, oregano and thyme in a large bowl and stir to combine.

Meanwhile, bring a large pot of water to a boil over medium-high heat. Add ¼ teaspoon sea salt. Stir in the pasta. Decrease the heat to medium-low and cook, stirring occasionally, until the pasta is cooked *al dente*. Drain the pasta. Pour the steaming hot pasta over the olive oil/herb mixture in the large bowl. Top with the roasted vegetables and toss gently to combine all of the ingredients. Add more olive oil if the pasta seems dry. Season with salt and pepper, to taste. Serve immediately.

Amount per serving, based on 4 servings: 476 Calories; 9g Fat; 1g Saturated fat; 17g Protein; 97mg Sodium; 86g Total Carbohydrate; 16g Sugars; 16g Fiber

Capellini with White Beans and Zucchini

EASE FACTOR **2**

This sauce prepares quickly because no sautéing is necessary. The olives add a real zing while the beans and zucchini give it substance. Perfect for capellini or spaghetti, it's delicious served over brown rice, millet or quinoa, too.

SAUCE

1 can (24 to 28 ounces) **crushed tomatoes**

1 can (15 ounces) **white beans,** drained and rinsed

1 medium **zucchini,** cut into 1-inch cubes

½ cup **sliced green olives,** with pimento

2 cloves **garlic,** minced

2 tablespoons **filtered or spring water**

1 teaspoon **Italian seasoning blend**

½ teaspoon **reduced-sodium tamari**

⅛ teaspoon **crushed red pepper flakes**

PASTA

¼ teaspoon **sea salt** (optional)

1 pound **whole-grain or gluten-free capellini** ("angel hair" pasta)

Put all of the sauce ingredients into a medium-sized saucepan. Cover and bring to a simmer over medium heat. Decrease the heat to medium-low, cover and cook, stirring occasionally, for about 30 minutes.

While the sauce cooks, bring a large pot of water to a boil over medium-high heat. Add ¼ teaspoon sea salt (optional). Stir in the capellini. Decrease the heat to medium-low and cook, stirring occasionally, until tender but firm. Drain the capellini and portion into six individual pasta bowls. Ladle the sauce over the top and serve immediately.

Amount per serving, based on 6 servings: 395 Calories; 4g Fat; 0g Saturated fat; 16g Protein; 456mg Sodium; 78g Total Carbohydrate; 3g Sugars; 8g Fiber

Spaghetti with Green Beans and Arugula

EASE FACTOR 2 MAKES 6 SERVINGS

This supremely fresh tasting farm-to-table style recipe gets a peppery punch from thinly sliced arugula. It works beautifully as a one-pot summer supper, taking under 20 minutes to prepare.

PASTA

¼ teaspoon sea salt (optional)

1 pound whole-grain spaghetti

2¼ cups cleaned, trimmed and chopped green beans (1- to 2-inch pieces)

SAUCE

3 cups chopped ripe tomatoes

2 cloves garlic, minced

¼ teaspoon sea salt, plus more as needed

⅛ teaspoon freshly ground black pepper, plus more as needed

2 tablespoons extra-virgin olive oil

4 to 5 cups thinly sliced arugula, cleaned and stemmed

3 tablespoons capers, plus more for garnish

1 teaspoon reduced-sodium tamari

Bring a large pot of water to a boil over medium-high heat. Add ¼ teaspoon salt (optional). Stir in the spaghetti. Decrease the heat to medium-low and cook, stirring occasionally, for about 3 minutes. Add the green beans and cook, stirring occasionally, for 6 to 8 minutes, or until the beans and spaghetti are both tender, but firm.

Meanwhile, to make the sauce, put the tomatoes, garlic, ¼ teaspoon salt and pepper in a bowl large enough to also accommodate the cooked spaghetti. Stir gently until well combined. Drizzle in 1 tablespoon of the olive oil and stir gently until the tomatoes are evenly coated. Add the arugula. Using clean hands, massage the tomatoes and arugula for about 10 seconds, so that the tomatoes release some of their juices and the arugula becomes tenderized. Stir in the capers and let the mixture stand while the spaghetti and green beans cook.

Drain the green beans and spaghetti and, while piping hot, add them to the tomato mixture. Drizzle with 1 tablespoon olive oil and the tamari and toss gently until thoroughly combined. Season with more salt and pepper, to taste. Serve immediately in wide pasta bowls, garnished with a few more capers, if desired.

Amount per serving, based on 6 servings: 335 Calories; 7g Fat; 1g Saturated fat; 11g Protein; 24g Sodium; 61g Total Carbohydrate; 6g Sugars; 10g Fiber

Mac 'n Peas with Creamy Butternut Squash Sauce

EASE FACTOR **3**   MAKES 6 SERVINGS

Craving the comforting, creamy texture and smooth taste of mac and cheese? This innovative recipe fills the bill when you're seeking a warm and hearty replacement for that dairy-laden version. Peas add color and pop, while the butternut squash and cashews create a super velvety sauce.

3¾ cups peeled, seeded and coarsely chopped butternut squash

2 small cloves garlic, chopped

⅓ cup raw cashews

½ cup plus 1½ tablespoons filtered or spring water, plus more as needed

¾ teaspoon sea salt, plus more as needed

1 pound whole-wheat or whole-grain fusilli, elbow or *chiocciole* pasta

1 cup frozen peas, thawed

¼ teaspoon dry mustard powder

¼ teaspoon smoked paprika

⅛ teaspoon cayenne pepper

⅛ teaspoon ground turmeric

Freshly ground pepper, to taste

♪ **Chef's Note** The butternut squash and garlic may be steamed in advance of preparing this recipe. After steaming, cool and store tightly covered in the refrigerator for up to 24 hours.

Photo courtesy of Annie Oliverio. Learn more about Annie on page 249.

Amount per serving, based on 6 servings: 310 Calories; 3g Fat; 0g Saturated fat; 12g Protein; 4mg Sodium; 63g Total Carbohydrate; 11g Sugars; 5g Fiber

Fit a steamer basket into a medium-sized saucepan with a tight-fitting lid. Add 2 to 3 inches of cold water to the pot and then add the butternut squash and garlic. Cover and bring to a boil. Steam the butternut squash and garlic until very tender, about 20 minutes. Let the butternut squash and garlic cool for about 20 minutes (see note).

Meanwhile, put the cashews and ½ cup water in a small bowl. Let soak for 30 to 40 minutes. Drain the soaking water from the cashews and thoroughly rinse the cashews under clean, cold running water.

Once the butternut squash and garlic have cooled, bring a large pot of water to a boil over medium-high heat. Add ¼ teaspoon salt (optional). Stir in the pasta. Decrease the heat to medium-low and cook, stirring occasionally, until the pasta is almost tender. Add the peas and cook, stirring occasionally, until the pasta is tender but firm and the peas are heated through, about 3 minutes. Drain the pasta and peas.

While the pasta and peas cook, put the cooled butternut squash and garlic, cashews, 1½ tablespoons of cold water, mustard powder, smoked paprika, ½ teaspoon salt, cayenne pepper and turmeric into a blender and process until the consistency of a thick, smooth sauce. Add more water 1 tablespoon at a time, as needed, to achieve the desired consistency. Transfer the sauce to a medium-sized pan and cook over medium-low heat, just until heated through, stirring often and adding more water as needed if the sauce is too thick.

Put the pasta and peas in a large bowl. Immediately pour the warm sauce over the pasta and gently stir to combine. Season with salt and pepper, to taste. Serve hot.

Seitan and Summer Squash Lasagna

This light and satisfying twist on an old favorite makes an impressive summer supper. The seitan adds a meaty flavor, the squash stands in beautifully for wheat noodles and the tofu provides a "cheesy" taste. Perfect for a family meal or casual dinner party.

1 block (14 to 15 ounces) firm regular tofu, drained

⅓ cup chopped fresh basil

2 cloves garlic, minced

1 teaspoon reduced-sodium tamari

⅛ teaspoon cayenne pepper

1 jar (26 to 28 ounces) vegan marinara sauce

3 medium yellow summer squash or zucchini, sliced lengthwise into ⅛- to ¼-inch wide "noodles"

1 package (8 ounces) crumbled or ground seitan

8 ounces cremini mushrooms, sliced

4 slices whole-grain bread, torn into chunks

1 tablespoon all-purpose seasoning blend

½ teaspoon sea salt

1½ tablespoons extra-virgin olive oil

Chef's Note 1 cup of shredded vegan cheese can be used in place of the bread crumbs, if desired.

Amount per serving, based on 6 servings: 352 Calories; 10g Fat; 2g Saturated fat; 25g Protein; 596mg Sodium; 40g Total Carbohydrate; 9g Sugars; 4g Fiber

P reheat the oven to 400 degrees F.

Put the tofu, basil, garlic, tamari and cayenne pepper in a medium-sized bowl and mash with a potato masher until the mixture has the consistency of ricotta cheese. Set aside.

Spread one cup of the marinara sauce in the bottom of a 9 x 12-inch casserole dish. Top with one-third of the squash "noodles" arranged in a single layer over the sauce. Top the squash with all of the seitan and ½ cup of the marinara sauce.

Arrange one-third of the squash "noodles" in a single layer over the seitan. Spread the tofu mixture in an even layer over the squash. Sprinkle about two-thirds of the sliced mushrooms over the tofu mixture and top them with ½ cup marinara sauce.

Arrange the remaining squash "noodles" over the marinara sauce. Dice the remaining sliced mushrooms and put them in a small bowl with ¾ cup marinara sauce. Stir to combine. Spread the diced mushroom-marinara mixture in an even layer over the squash. Tent with foil and bake for 40 minutes.

While the lasagna bakes, put the bread chunks, all-purpose seasoning and salt in a blender and process into coarse crumbs. Transfer the crumbs to a medium-sized bowl. Add the olive oil and stir to coat.

Remove the foil and top the lasagna with the bread crumb mixture (see note). Cover and bake for 15 minutes. Remove the foil and bake uncovered for 7 to 10 minutes, or until the lasagna is bubbling and the bread crumb topping is golden and crisp. Let cool 12 to 15 minutes before cutting the lasagna into squares for serving.

White Lasagna with Mushrooms and Green Peas

EASE FACTOR ❸   **MAKES 6 SERVINGS**

Creamy, with a rich, dairy-free white sauce, this lasagna offers a welcome change to the red sauce that is characteristically associated with this classic dish. This is a fancier, more complex lasagna, accented with colorful green peas and earthy mushrooms. There *are* quite a few steps in this recipe, but it's well worth it if you are looking for an impressive dish to serve at an elegant dinner party!

WHITE SAUCE

8½ cups cauliflower florets

2 cups peeled and diced yellow potatoes

½ cup diced sweet onion

1 clove garlic, chopped

½ teaspoon sea salt

Several grinds of freshly ground black pepper

¾ cup unsweetened nondairy milk, plus more as needed

NOODLES

1/4 teaspoon sea salt (optional)

12 whole-grain lasagna noodles

MUSHROOM-ONION SAUCE

2¼ cups diced sweet onion

8 ounces thinly sliced cremini mushrooms

¼ cup filtered or spring water, plus more as needed

1½ teaspoons dried basil

1 teaspoon reduced-sodium tamari

1 teaspoon extra-virgin olive oil

Amount per serving, based on 6 servings: 421 Calories; 6g Fat; 1g Saturated fat; 18g Protein; 153mg Sodium; 77g Total Carbohydrate; 16g Sugars; 14g Fiber

Preheat the oven to 375 degrees F.

Fit a steamer basket into a large pot with a tight-fitting lid. Add 2 to 3 inches of cold water to the pot and then add the cauliflower and potatoes. Cover, bring to a boil, and steam for 25 minutes, or until the cauliflower and potatoes are soft. Let cool for 20 to 30 minutes.

Meanwhile, to prepare the noodles, bring a large pot of water to a boil over medium-high heat. Add ¼ teaspoon salt (optional). Stir in the noodles a few at a time. Decrease the heat to medium-low and cook, stirring occasionally, until the noodles are cooked *al dente*. Drain and rinse under cool water, then drain again. Arrange the noodles in a single layer on a large baking sheet lined with unbleached parchment paper, so they do not stick together (see note).

To make the mushroom-onion sauce, put 2¼ cups diced sweet onions, mushrooms, water, basil, tamari and 1 teaspoon olive oil in a medium-sized skillet over medium-low heat. Cover and cook, stirring occasionally, for 7 to 8 minutes, until softened.

While the mushroom-onion sauce cooks, make the white sauce. Put the cooled cauliflower and potatoes into a large bowl. Add ½ cup sweet onion, garlic, salt and pepper; stir gently to combine. Put half of the cauliflower/potato mixture into a blender. Add about half of the nondairy milk and process until it is a smooth white sauce. Transfer to a large bowl. Repeat with the remaining cauliflower/potato mixture and nondairy milk. Transfer to the bowl. If the mixture is too thick, stir in more nondairy milk until the consistency resembles that of a classic white sauce.

ADDITIONAL INGREDIENTS

1 teaspoon extra-virgin olive oil

2 cups frozen peas, slightly thawed

BREAD CRUMB TOPPING

4 slices whole-grain bread, torn into chunks

1 teaspoon Italian seasoning blend

¼ teaspoon sea salt

2 teaspoons extra-virgin olive oil

Chef's Note You can cook the noodles up to 1 day in advance. Once they're cooked, spread them out on a baking sheet between layers of parchment paper. Then, wrap the baking sheet tightly in plastic wrap and refrigerate until you assemble the lasagna.

Spread one-quarter of the white sauce evenly over the bottom of a 9 x 12-inch casserole dish. Add 1 teaspoon of olive oil and stir to combine. Arrange four lasagna noodles over the white sauce. Spread another one-quarter of the white sauce evenly over the noodles. Spoon one-half of the mushroom-onion sauce over the white sauce in an even layer. Top with 1 cup of peas.

Arrange four lasagna noodles over the peas. Spread one-quarter of the white sauce evenly over the noodles. Spoon the remaining mushroom-onion sauce over the white sauce in an even layer. Top with the remaining peas.

Arrange 4 more noodles over the last layer of peas. Spread the remaining white sauce over the noodles. Cover (or tent with foil) and bake for 50 to 55 minutes.

While the lasagna bakes, put the bread chunks, Italian seasoning and salt in a blender and process into coarse crumbs. Put the bread crumb mixture in a small bowl. Add 2 teaspoons of olive oil and stir to combine.

Take the lasagna out of the oven and remove the cover. Sprinkle the bread crumb mixture evenly over the top. Cover and bake for 10 minutes. Uncover and bake for 10 to 15 minutes more, or until the bread crumbs are crispy and golden, and the lasagna is bubbling.

Let cool for 15 minutes. Cut into squares and proudly serve!

Vegan-*Ease* Pizza

EASE FACTOR ❶   MAKES 1 TO 2 SERVINGS

Easy and so delicious, this round pizza cuts corners by using a whole-grain sandwich wrap instead of pizza dough. The result is a crisp crust, topped with a mouthwatering combination of toppings, ready to eat in less than 20 minutes. Ideal to serve for a quick lunch or light supper.

1 10-inch whole-grain sandwich wrap or tortilla

2 to 3 tablespoons low-fat prepared marinara sauce

¼ teaspoon Italian seasoning blend

⅛ teaspoon crushed red pepper

2 cups lightly packed baby spinach, washed and dried

4 green queen olives with pimento, sliced (see note)

10 to 12 slices vegan pepperoni or 4 very thinly sliced cremini mushrooms

⅓ cup shredded vegan cheese (optional)

 reheat the oven to 400 degrees F.

Put the sandwich wrap on a large baking sheet or pizza pan. Spread the marinara sauce over the wrap, in an even layer, leaving a slight margin around the edge for a "crust." Sprinkle the Italian seasoning and crushed pepper over the sauce. Top with the baby spinach, pressing it down to make it more compact.

Top with the olives, vegan pepperoni (or mushrooms) and vegan cheese (optional). Bake for 10 to 12 minutes, or until crust is crisp and toppings are heated through. Cut into wedges and serve.

> **Chef's Note** Pitted Kalamata olives may be used in place of the green olives.

Amount per serving, based on 2 servings: 167 Calories; 4g Fat; 0g Saturated fat; 8g Protein; 357mg Sodium; 25g Total Carbohydrate; 3g Sugars; 5g Fiber

Nutritional Information with optional vegan cheese: Amount per serving, based on 2 servings: 226 Calories; 8g Fat; 2g Saturated fat; 9g Protein; 522mg Sodium; 29g Total Carbohydrate; 3g Sugars; 6g Fiber

Rápido Mexican Pizza

EASE FACTOR ❷

MAKES 4 SERVINGS

Sometimes you just crave Mexican flavors and when you do, these thin, crispy crust individual pizzas are the perfect choice. *Viva the vegan pizza!*

CHICKPEA "CHEESE"

1 can (15 ounces) chickpeas (garbanzo beans), drained and rinsed

4 heaping tablespoons prepared salsa

¼ teaspoon chili powder

¼ teaspoon garlic powder

⅛ teaspoon ground cumin

⅛ teaspoon ground turmeric

CRUST

4 8-inch whole-grain tortillas

ADDITIONAL TOPPINGS

4 tablespoons prepared salsa

4 cups lightly packed mixed spring salad greens

10 green queen olives with pimento, chopped

1 cup shredded vegan cheese (optional)

Preheat the oven to 375 degrees F. Line one extra-large (or two medium-sized) rimmed baking sheet(s) with unbleached parchment paper.

Put the chickpea "cheese" ingredients in a medium-sized bowl and mash using a potato masher or large fork until the consistency of large curd cottage cheese. Set aside.

Put the tortillas on the prepared baking sheet(s). Spread 1 tablespoon salsa in an even layer over a tortilla, leaving a slight margin around the edge for a "crust." Spread one-quarter of the chickpea "cheese" over the salsa in an even layer. Add 1 cup mixed spring greens and press down to compress. Sprinkle one-quarter of the chopped olives over the top. Repeat in the same manner with the three remaining tortillas.

Bake for 15 minutes. Remove from the oven and sprinkle the top of each pizza with vegan cheese (optional). Bake for 5 minutes, or until the vegan cheese (optional) is melted, the crust is crisp and toppings are heated through. Serve hot.

Amount per serving, based on 4 servings: 294 Calories; 6g Fat; 1g Saturated fat; 12g Protein; 913mg Sodium; 53g Total Carbohydrate; 4g Sugars; 1g Fiber

Nutritional Information with optional vegan cheese: Amount per serving, based on 4 servings: 384 Calories; 12g Fat; 3g Saturated fat; 13g Protein; 1163mg Sodium; 60g Total Carbohydrate; 4g Sugars; 11g Fiber

These vegan versions of traditional favorites like burgers, casseroles and cutlets prove that plant power can be tasty and satisfying for everyone.

the main dish made *ease-y*

Facing page: "Hungry Guy" Burgers, page 132

This satisfying "cutlet" recipe makes sophisticated use of the humble cauliflower, giving it some serious *wow* factor! Easy to double or triple, this recipe makes a fancy weeknight main dish or elegant entrée for a party.

Roasted Cauliflower Cutlets with Lemon-Caper Sauce

EASE FACTOR ❷   **MAKES 4 SERVINGS**

1 medium head of cauliflower

2 tablespoons plus 1 teaspoon extra-virgin olive oil (see note)

1½ teaspoons Italian seasoning blend

¾ teaspoon garlic powder

1 medium sweet onion, thinly sliced

1 cup vegetable broth, plus more as needed

3 tablespoons freshly squeezed lemon juice (from about 1½ lemons; zest one of the lemons first, before squeezing)

2 tablespoons capers, drained and rinsed

Zest of one lemon, for garnish

2 tablespoons chopped fresh parsley for garnish (optional)

Chef's Note To lower the fat content of this recipe, you may use vegetable broth in place of the olive oil.

Preheat the oven to 375 degrees F. Line a large, rimmed baking sheet with unbleached parchment paper.

Trim one to two inches off the two opposite sides of the cauliflower head, and set aside for another use. Cut the cauliflower head into four, ¾- to 1-inch thick "cutlets," as if slicing a loaf of bread. Arrange the cutlets in a single layer on the prepared baking sheet.

Put 2 tablespoons extra-virgin olive oil, 1 teaspoon Italian seasoning and ½ teaspoon garlic powder in a small bowl and whisk to combine. Liberally spread one-quarter of the seasoning mixture over the top of each cutlet, using a small pastry brush or back of a small spoon. Bake for 35 to 40 minutes, or until tender and slightly golden brown around the edges.

To make the sauce, put the onion and ½ cup vegetable broth in a large skillet. Cover and cook over medium-low heat for 7 to 10 minutes, or until the onion has softened. Add ½ teaspoon Italian seasoning blend, ¼ teaspoon garlic powder and another ½ cup vegetable broth, cover and cook, stirring occasionally, for 10 minutes. If the onions become dry, add more broth, 2 tablespoons at a time. Stir in 1 teaspoon olive oil, lemon juice and capers. Cover and cook, stirring occasionally, for about 2 minutes, or until the capers are heated through.

To serve, put each cutlet on a dinner plate and spoon one-quarter of the onion-caper sauce over each cutlet. Garnish with lemon zest and parsley. Serve warm.

Amount per serving, based on 4 servings: 108 Calories; 9g Fat; 1g Saturated fat; 3g Protein; 227mg Sodium; 8g Total Carbohydrate; 3g Sugars; 3g Fiber

Photo courtesy of Annie Oliverio. Learn more about Annie on page 249.

These yummy little eggplant stacks are filled with a tasty homemade vegan "cheese" and topped with a spicy tomato sauce, making an excellent choice for a casual supper or dinner party.

Eggplant Stack-Ups

EASE FACTOR ❸   MAKES 6 SERVINGS

1 can (28 ounces) diced tomatoes, with juice

1½ teaspoons Italian seasoning blend

3 teaspoons extra-virgin olive oil, plus more as needed

¼ teaspoon garlic powder

¼ teaspoon dried crushed rosemary

¼ teaspoon cayenne pepper

1 very large or 2 medium eggplants

1 can (15 ounces) white beans, drained and rinsed

⅓ cup raw cashews

⅓ cup filtered or spring water

1 clove garlic, chopped

½ teaspoon sea salt

3 slices whole-grain bread, torn into chunks

Preheat the oven to 400 degrees F.

To make the tomato sauce, put the tomatoes (with juice), 1 teaspoon Italian seasoning, 1 teaspoon olive oil, garlic powder, rosemary and ⅛ teaspoon cayenne pepper in a medium-sized bowl and stir to combine. Trim off the stem end of the eggplant(s) and discard. Cut a 1½- to 2-inch slice off each end of the eggplant(s) and dice. Add the diced eggplant to the tomato sauce and stir to combine.

Slice the center of the eggplant(s) into ⅛- to ¼-inch wide slices, to make 24 slices.

Next, put the white beans, cashews, water, chopped garlic, ¼ teaspoon sea salt and ⅛ teaspoon cayenne pepper in a blender and process until smooth.

Spread half of the tomato sauce mixture evenly in the bottom of a 9 x 12-inch casserole dish. Spread a heaping tablespoon of the cashew mixture evenly on each of 6 eggplant slices. Arrange the 6 slices in a single layer over the top of the tomato sauce in the casserole dish. Spread a heaping tablespoon of the cashew mixture evenly on 6 more eggplant slices. Arrange these 6 slices over the first layer of slices, to start assembling the "stacks." Continue in this manner with 6 more eggplant slices. Top each stack with a plain eggplant slice. (There will be 4 slices of eggplant in each of 6 stacks). Top each stack with one-sixth of the remaining tomato sauce mixture.

Amount per serving, based on 6 servings: 199 Calories; 4g Fat; 1g Saturated fat; 9g Protein; 274mg Sodium; 33g Total Carbohydrate; 8g Sugars; 9g Fiber

Cover and bake for 50 to 60 minutes, or until the eggplant is almost soft.

While the eggplant bakes, put the whole-grain bread chunks, ½ teaspoon Italian seasoning and ¼ teaspoon salt in a blender and pulse on medium-low to process into coarse crumbs. Put the crumbs in a small bowl and add 2 teaspoons olive oil. Gently toss to evenly coat the bread crumbs with the oil. If the bread crumbs still seem dry, add 1 more teaspoon of olive oil and stir to coat.

Remove the cover from the casserole and sprinkle one-sixth of the bread crumb mixture over the top of each stack. Cover and bake for 10 minutes. Uncover and bake for 5 to 10 minutes more or until the eggplant is soft, the crumbs are golden and the sauce is bubbling. Cool 10 minutes. Serve one stack per person with rice, quinoa or whole-grain pasta served on the side.

These meaty-tasting mushrooms are filled to the brim with hearty quinoa, walnuts, sweet red peppers and fresh basil, making them a colorful, crowd-pleasing entrée. Bonus: They are gluten-free *and* soy-free, ideal when entertaining guests with these common dietary restrictions.

Walnut and Quinoa Stuffed Portobello Mushrooms

EASE FACTOR **3**   **MAKES 6 TO 8 SERVINGS**

1 cup uncooked quinoa, thoroughly rinsed and drained

2 cups water

½ vegan bouillon cube

8 portobello mushrooms, stems removed

2 tablespoons plus 2 teaspoons extra-virgin olive oil

¼ teaspoon sea salt, plus more as needed

⅔ cup diced sweet red pepper

⅔ cup walnut halves, chopped

½ cup chopped fresh basil

⅓ cup roasted and salted cashews, chopped

2 cloves garlic, minced

3 tablespoons capers, drained and rinsed

2 teaspoons all-purpose seasoning blend

⅛ teaspoon freshly ground pepper

Put the quinoa in a saucepan with the water and bouillon cube. Cover and bring to a simmer over medium-low heat. Cook for 15 to 17 minutes, or until all the water is absorbed. Fluff with a fork, remove from heat and let cool for 20 to 30 minutes (see note).

Preheat the oven to 400 degrees F. Line a large, rimmed baking pan with unbleached parchment paper.

Put the mushrooms gill side up on the prepared pan. Drizzle ½ teaspoon olive oil and a dash of sea salt over the gills of each mushroom.

Put the cooled quinoa, sweet red pepper, walnuts, basil, cashews, garlic, capers, all-purpose seasoning, ⅛ teaspoon salt and pepper in a large bowl. Stir gently with a large spoon to combine. Put ⅓ heaping cup of the quinoa mixture into each mushroom, patting it down firmly as you go. Brush the top of the quinoa mixture on each mushroom with about ½ teaspoon olive oil, using a pastry brush or back of a small spoon.

Tent the mushrooms with foil. Bake for 50 minutes, or until the mushrooms are soft.

Remove foil from the mushrooms and bake uncovered for 10 to 15 minutes, or until the top of the stuffing gets slightly golden. Put the pan on a wire rack and cool for 10 minutes before serving.

 Chef's Note You can cook the quinoa up to 1 day in advance. Once cooked, cool the quinoa, cover tightly and refrigerate until you are ready to stuff the mushrooms.

Amount per serving, based on 8 servings: 315 Calories; 22g Fat; 3g Saturated fat; 9g Protein; 42mg Sodium; 23g Total Carbohydrate; 3g Sugars; 5g Fiber

I used to *love* crab cakes and creating a vegan version has been high on my "to-do" list for quite a while. So imagine my happy dance when I came up with this authentic-tasting adaptation that is so easy to prepare! These cakes make an appetizing first course or main dish for any special meal, served with a zingy sauce on the side.

Not-So-Crabby Cakes with Classic Cocktail Sauce

EASE FACTOR ❸   MAKES 8 CAKES

CLASSIC COCKTAIL SAUCE

¼ cup catsup

1½ tablespoons prepared horseradish, plus more as needed

1 teaspoon freshly squeezed lemon juice

"CRABBY" CAKES

2¼ cups lightly packed fresh soft bread crumbs (see note)

1 teaspoon dry mustard powder

½ teaspoon dried marjoram

¼ teaspoon sea salt

¼ teaspoon cayenne pepper (use ⅛ teaspoon for less heat)

¼ teaspoon dulse flakes or granules (optional, see note)

1 cup firmly packed grated zucchini

½ cup minced fresh onion

3 heaping tablespoons sesame tahini, plus more as needed

BREADING

⅔ cup lightly packed fresh soft bread crumbs

2 teaspoons extra-virgin olive oil, plus more as needed

¼ teaspoon sea salt

GARNISH

4 lemon wedges

Put all of the sauce ingredients in a small bowl. Stir to combine. Taste and add more horseradish, if desired. Cover and refrigerate until serving.

Preheat the oven to 400 degrees F. Line a large, rimmed baking sheet with unbleached parchment paper.

To make the cakes, put 2¼ cups bread crumbs, mustard powder, marjoram, ¼ teaspoon sea salt, cayenne pepper and dulse (optional) in a large bowl and stir with a large spoon to combine. Add the zucchini and onion and gently stir to combine. Add the tahini and stir well, mixing it into the zucchini mixture until completely incorporated. If the mixture still seems dry, add 1 more heaping tablespoon of tahini.

To make the breading, put ⅔ cup bread crumbs, 2 teaspoons olive oil and ¼ teaspoon sea salt in a small bowl and stir to combine. Add an additional teaspoon of olive oil if the bread crumbs seem dry.

Scoop up ¼ cup of the zucchini mixture and form it into a cake. Dip it in the breading mixture to thoroughly coat both sides. Put the cake on the prepared baking sheet. Gently press down on the cake to compress it slightly. (This will help it to hold together while baking). Continue in this manner to form a total of eight cakes.

Tent loosely with foil and bake for 20 to 25 minutes, or until the cakes begin to get golden around the edges. Flip the cakes and re-tent with the foil. Bake for 10 to 15 more minutes, or until slightly golden. Remove the foil and bake for another 5 to 7 minutes or until the cakes are crispy and golden brown. Put the sheet on a wire rack and let cool 5 minutes. The

cakes will be slightly soft. To serve, carefully transfer the cakes, using a flat spatula, onto individual serving plates.

For an appetizer, serve one cake per person; for a main course, serve two to three cakes per person, with Classic Cocktail Sauce on the side and garnished with a lemon wedge.

Chef's Notes

- Freshly made bread crumbs *must* be used in this recipe, as dry bread crumbs will not hold the cakes together. To make fresh bread crumbs, tear 6 to 8 slices of fresh, soft, whole-grain bread into chunks. Put one-third of the bread chunks in a blender. Process (on low) into coarse crumbs. Continue in this way with the remaining bread chunks.

- If you cannot find dulse flakes or granules, you may use nori instead. Put a $^1/_2$ sheet of toasted nori into a blender and grind into coarse crumbs. Proceed with recipe as directed.

Amount per serving, based on 8 servings/cakes: 195 Calories; 6g Fat; 1g Saturated fat; 6g Protein; 328mg Sodium; 28g Total Carbohydrate; 5g Sugars; 2g Fiber

My husband always complained that I did not make our veggie burgers BIG enough! So the "Hungry Guy" Burger was born. Packed with hearty black beans, spicy salsa and rolled oats, these five-ingredient wonders are filling and super-quick to prepare. Now everyone's happy!

"Hungry Guy" Burgers

EASE FACTOR ❶   *MAKES 6 BURGERS*

1 can (15 ounces) black beans, drained and rinsed

⅔ cup plus 2 heaping tablespoons prepared salsa, plus more as needed (see note)

3 slices whole-grain bread, torn into chunks

¼ teaspoon ground cumin

⅔ cup rolled oats

P reheat the oven to 375 degrees F. Line a large, rimmed baking pan with unbleached parchment paper.

Put the black beans and salsa in a medium-sized bowl and mash using a potato masher or large fork until well combined. Put the bread chunks and cumin in a blender and process into coarse crumbs. Add the bread crumbs to the black bean mixture and stir to combine. Stir in the rolled oats and mix to combine. If the mixture seems dry, stir in another heaping tablespoon of salsa and mix to combine.

Scoop up a generous ½ cup of the black bean mixture and put it on the prepared pan. Form it into a burger, shaping it with clean hands, then flattening it slightly. Continue in this manner to make five more burgers (see note). Bake for 20 minutes. Flip the burgers and bake for 8 to 12 minutes, or until golden.

Chef's Notes

- You may use mild, medium or hot salsa in this recipe.
- Once formed, the burgers may be covered and refrigerated for 2 to 6 hours before cooking. Add 5 to 7 minutes to the baking time.

Photo courtesy of Annie Oliverio. Learn more about Annie on page 249.

Amount per serving, based on 6 servings/burgers: 170 Calories; 2g Fat; 0g Saturated fat; 10g Protein; 241mg Sodium; 30g Total Carbohydrate; 1g Sugars; 8g Fiber

These beautiful patties are simple to make, using leftover brown rice. Tasting like a cross between falafel and a veggie burger, they make a nice luncheon entrée or light supper.

Chickpea-Brown Rice Patties

EASE FACTOR   **MAKES 6 TO 7 PATTIES**

BREADING

1 cup lightly packed fresh whole-grain bread crumbs (see note)

2 teaspoons extra-virgin olive oil

¼ teaspoon sea salt

PATTIES

1 can (15 ounces) chickpeas (garbanzo beans), drained and rinsed

1 cup firmly packed cooked short-grain brown rice

2 tablespoons prepared catsup

1 teaspoon chili powder

1 cup lightly packed fresh whole-grain bread crumbs

Preheat the oven to 400 degrees F. Line a large, rimmed baking sheet with unbleached parchment paper.

To make the breading, put 1 cup bread crumbs, 2 teaspoons olive oil and sea salt in a small bowl and stir to combine.

To make the patties, put the chickpeas, brown rice, catsup and chili powder in a large bowl and coarsely mash with a potato masher or large fork. Add 1 cup bread crumbs and stir until incorporated. Scoop up a heaping ⅓ cup of the chickpea mixture and form it into a patty. Dip it in the breading mixture to thoroughly coat. Put the patty on the prepared baking sheet. Continue in this manner to form six to seven patties in all. Tent loosely with foil and bake for 25 minutes. Flip the patties and tent again. Bake for 15 minutes more. Remove the foil and bake for 3 to 5 minutes, or until the patties are crispy and golden. Put the pan on a wire rack and let cool 5 minutes. The patties will be slightly soft. To serve, carefully transfer the patties onto individual serving plates. Serve with a green salad and Classic Cocktail Sauce (page 130).

Chef's Note

To make fresh bread crumbs, tear about 4 slices of whole-grain bread into chunks. Put the chunks in a blender and process into coarse crumbs.

Amount per serving, based on 7 servings/patties: 273 Calories; 3g Fat; 0g Saturated fat; 8g Protein; 465mg Sodium; 53g Total Carbohydrate; 3g Sugars; 8g Fiber

Traditional paella is rice-based, but here it's kicked up a notch with protein-packed quinoa. The result is a filling and flavorful paella-style dish that makes for a guest-worthy meal. Even though there *are* a lot of ingredients, there is no pre-sautéing required, allowing this dish to come together quickly.

Quinoa and Butternut Squash Paella

EASE FACTOR ❸   MAKES 8 TO 10 SERVINGS

1 can (28 ounces) whole peeled tomatoes, with liquid

1½ cups diced onion

4 cups chopped butternut squash (cut into 1-inch cubes)

1 can (15 ounces) chickpeas (garbanzo beans), drained and rinsed

1½ cups lightly packed, thinly sliced curly kale

1¾ cups uncooked quinoa, thoroughly rinsed and drained

2½ cups vegetable broth, plus more as needed

2 cloves garlic, minced

2 teaspoons brown sugar (optional)

2 teaspoons freshly squeezed lemon juice

1 teaspoon ground turmeric

½ teaspoon smoked or sweet paprika

½ teaspoon sea salt

⅛ teaspoon cayenne pepper

1 large red pepper, sliced into strips

Lemon wedges, for garnish

2 to 3 scallions, chopped, for garnish

our the tomatoes and their juice in a medium-sized bowl and lightly mash, using a potato masher or large fork. Put the onion and tomatoes in a 12-inch paella pan or large, deep skillet. Cover and bring to a simmer over medium heat. Decrease the heat to medium-low, cover and cook for 5 minutes. Stir in the butternut squash, cover and cook for 15 minutes, stirring occasionally. Stir in the chickpeas, kale and quinoa. Cover and cook for 2 minutes.

Put the broth, garlic, sugar (optional), lemon juice, turmeric, paprika, salt and cayenne pepper in a medium-sized bowl and stir to incorporate. Pour the broth mixture into the skillet and gently stir to combine. Cover and cook for 30 minutes, stirring every 10 minutes. If the pan seems dry, add 3 tablespoons of vegetable broth at a time, as needed, to keep the paella moist. Stir the paella one more time and then arrange the red pepper slices over the top of the paella in a pretty pattern. *Do not stir.*

Decrease the heat to low, cover and cook for 10 to 15 minutes, or until all of the liquid is absorbed. Remove from the heat and allow the paella to stand for 10 to 15 minutes.

Sprinkle the scallions over the top and serve family style, or portion out the paella and serve on individual plates with a lemon wedge on the side.

Amount per serving, based on 10 servings: 226 Calories; 3g Fat; 0g Saturated fat; 8g Protein; 410mg Sodium; 44g Total Carbohydrate; 5g Sugars; 6g Fiber

This elegant, flavorful and meaty-tasting dish prepares in 15 minutes from start to finish, making it an ideal entrée to serve at any gathering when you're short on time.

Seitan Piccata

EASE FACTOR **1**

16 ounces seitan, drained and sliced or cubed

1 cup vegetable broth

1 teaspoon all-purpose seasoning blend

Dash cayenne pepper

1 large lemon, sliced in half

2 tablespoons capers, drained and rinsed

Sea salt, to taste

Freshly ground pepper, to taste

Chopped fresh flat-leaf parsley, for garnish

Put the seitan, vegetable broth, all-purpose seasoning and cayenne pepper in a large skillet. Bring to a simmer, cover and cook over medium-low heat, stirring occasionally, for 5 minutes.

Meanwhile, squeeze 1½ to 2 tablespoons juice from half the lemon. Cut the remaining lemon half into 4 wedges and set aside.

Add 1 tablespoon of the lemon juice and the capers to the skillet. Cover and cook 5 minutes, stirring occasionally. Taste and add more lemon juice, if desired. Season with salt and pepper, to taste. To serve, spoon over cooked rice, pasta or quinoa. Garnish with parsley and serve with a lemon wedge on the side.

 Watch Laura Theodore make this recipe at vegan-ease.com

Amount per serving, based on 4 servings: 161 Calories; 3g Fat; 0g Saturated fat; 28g Protein; 689mg Sodium; 7g Total Carbohydrate; 3g Sugars; 1g Fiber

Constant stirring is not required, making this an easy risotto to prepare for a quick weeknight meal. Summer squash stands in well for the cheese, adding color and creaminess. Just chop up a few key ingredients, give it an occasional stir, and it's ready to serve!

Mushroom and Summer Squash Risotto

EASE FACTOR **2**   MAKES 2 TO 3 SERVINGS

²/₃ cup diced onion

8 ounces cremini or white button mushrooms, chopped

3 cups filtered or spring water, plus more as needed

1 vegan bouillon cube, crumbled

1 cup Arborio rice

½ cup peeled and diced yellow summer squash

Chopped fresh flat leaf parsley, for garnish

ut the onion, mushrooms, ½ cup water and crumbled bouillon cube into a medium-sized saucepan. Cover and cook over medium heat, stirring occasionally, about 7 minutes, or until soft. Add more water, 2 tablespoons at a time, if needed, to prevent sticking.

Decrease the heat to medium-low (or low) and add 1 cup of the water to the onion-mushroom mixture. Stir in the rice, cover and cook for 7 to 8 minutes, or until the water is almost absorbed. Stir the risotto thoroughly; add 1 more cup of water, cover and cook for 8 to 10 more minutes, or until the water is almost completely absorbed.

Stir the risotto again, then stir in ½ cup water and the squash. Cover and cook 8 to 10 minutes, or until the squash is very soft and water is almost fully absorbed. Stir again. Remove the risotto from the heat, cover and let stand for 7 to 10 minutes to allow the remaining water to be absorbed, stirring one last time. Garnish with parsley; serve warm.

Amount per serving, based on 3 servings: 279 Calories; 2g Fat; 1g Saturated fat; 9g Protein; 106mg Sodium; 55g Total Carbohydrate; 4g Sugars; 3g Fiber

This delightfully fragrant and satisfying stew makes impressive fare for company. The garlic adds real pizzazz without overwhelming the other ingredients. Make this dish the star of your menu on a chilly late summer evening or cold autumn night.

Lentil, Brown Rice and Carrot Stew

EASE FACTOR ③　　　　　　　　　　　　　　　　**MAKES 6 TO 8 SERVINGS**

4½ cups cubed zucchini (cut in 1- to 1½-inch cubes)

2 cups chopped fresh tomatoes

1⅔ cups sliced carrots

1 cup long-grain brown rice, rinsed

1 cup green lentils, sorted, cleaned and rinsed

1 small sweet onion, chopped

¼ cup sliced fresh garlic

2 large vegan bouillon cubes

1½ teaspoons reduced-sodium tamari

10 cups filtered or spring water

3 cups lightly packed, thinly sliced kale

¼ cup chopped fresh basil

Sea salt, to taste

Freshly ground pepper, to taste

Put the zucchini, tomatoes, carrots, rice, lentils, onion, garlic, bouillon cubes and tamari in a large soup pot. Pour in the water and stir to combine. Cover and cook over medium-low heat, stirring occasionally, for 40 minutes. Add the kale, cover and cook, stirring occasionally, for 20 minutes. Add the basil and cook for 5 to 10 minutes, or until the lentils and rice are soft. Season with salt and pepper, to taste.

Serve hot with crusty whole-grain bread and a crisp green salad on the side.

Amount per serving, based on 8 servings: 167 Calories; 2g Fat; 1g Saturated fat; 9g Protein; 549mg Sodium; 31g Total Carbohydrate; 7g Sugars; 5g Fiber

A colorful side dish made from fresh produce
provides an essential accompaniment
to a well-rounded meal.

sunny sides

11

Facing page: Zingy Roasted Asparagus, page 155

Escarole with Kalamata Olives

EASE FACTOR ❶

I adore the taste of spicy escarole combined with zippy Kalamata olives. This tasty side holds its own served with just about anything.

1 large bunch escarole, washed and coarsely chopped

1 cup pitted Kalamata olives

3 small cloves garlic, minced

2 tablespoons water, plus more as needed

⅛ teaspoon crushed red pepper flakes

1 tablespoon freshly squeezed lemon juice

Put the escarole, olives, garlic, water and pepper flakes in a large skillet. Cover and cook over medium-low heat for 10 minutes, stirring frequently. If the skillet becomes dry, add water, 2 tablespoons at a time, to keep the escarole from sticking. Add the lemon juice, cover and cook 4 to 6 minutes, or until the escarole is wilted and olives are heated through.

Amount per serving, based on 4 servings: 153 Calories; 12g Fat; 0g Saturated fat; 1g Protein; 1120mg Sodium; 11g Total Carbohydrate; 1g Sugars; 2g Fiber

Baked Steak Fries, *above*   ·   Chili-Chickpea Stuffed Spuds *(page 160), below*

Chili-Chickpea Stuffed Spuds

EASE FACTOR **1**

These tempting delights make a filling side dish but they are hearty enough to serve as a light luncheon entrée, too. A few ingredients packed into a pre-baked potato shell make easy work of this satisfying side.

2 medium russet potatoes, baked (see note page 158)

¾ cup cooked chickpeas (garbanzo beans)

2 tablespoons nondairy milk, plus more as needed

1 teaspoon chili powder

¼ teaspoon sea salt, plus more as needed

⅓ cup diced sweet red peppers

½ teaspoon sweet paprika

Preheat the oven to 400 degrees F. Line a small, rimmed baking pan with unbleached parchment paper.

Slice each potato in half lengthwise. Carefully scoop out the pulp, using a teaspoon or grapefruit spoon, leaving about ¼-inch of the potato skin intact.

Put the potato pulp, chickpeas, nondairy milk, chili powder and salt in a medium-sized bowl and coarsely mash using a potato masher or large fork. Add a bit more nondairy milk, if the mixture seems dry. Fold in the red peppers. Stuff one-quarter of the potato pulp mixture into each potato skin.

Place the stuffed potato on the prepared baking pan. Repeat until all of the potato skins are filled. Sprinkle the tops of each potato with paprika. Tent with foil and bake for 30 minutes. Uncover and bake for 18 to 20 minutes, or until the tops are crispy and slightly golden. Cool for 5 to 7 minutes. Season with more salt, to taste. Serve warm.

Amount per serving, based on 4 servings: 141 Calories; 1g Fat; 0g Saturated fat; 5g Protein; 90mg Sodium; 28g Total Carbohydrate; 3g Sugars; 5g Fiber

Spicy Baked Home Fries

EASE FACTOR **1**   MAKES 4 SERVINGS

My husband loves home fries. So I came up with this tantalizing version that's easy to make for any meal of the day. There's a little heat and a lot of zest. Everybody loves 'em!

6 cups unpeeled, cubed russet potatoes (1-inch cubes)

2 medium sweet onions, sliced

1 tablespoon plus 1 teaspoon extra-virgin olive oil

½ tablespoon chili powder

1 teaspoon garlic powder

½ teaspoon sweet paprika

⅛ teaspoon cayenne pepper

¼ teaspoon sea salt, plus more to taste

Amount per serving, based on 4 servings: 248 Calories; 5g Fat; 1g Saturated fat; 6g Protein; 14mg Sodium; 48g Total Carbohydrate; 6g Sugars; 4g Fiber

Preheat the oven to 400 degrees F. Line a large, rimmed baking sheet with unbleached parchment paper.

Put the potatoes, onions and olive oil in a large bowl and toss to coat. Put the chili powder, garlic powder, paprika and cayenne pepper in a small bowl and stir to combine.

Add the spice mixture to the potatoes and onions and toss gently to coat.

Spread the potato and onion mixture in a single layer on the prepared baking sheet. Bake for 45 to 55 minutes, or until soft on the inside and golden on the outside, turning with a spatula halfway through baking. Cool slightly and add more salt, as desired. Serve warm.

This pudding makes good use of leftover brown rice. It takes only five minutes to prepare for the oven and serves double-duty as a lovely finish to a weeknight meal or even an appealing breakfast treat.

Five-Ingredient Rice Pudding

EASE FACTOR ❶   **MAKES 4 TO 6 SERVINGS**

2½ cups cooked short-grain brown rice

¾ cup nondairy milk

½ cup raisins

¼ cup maple syrup

¼ teaspoon ground cinnamon

Preheat the oven to 375 degrees F. Put the rice, nondairy milk, raisins and maple syrup in a medium-sized casserole dish and stir to combine. Sprinkle the cinnamon over the top. Cover and bake for 40 minutes, or until all of the liquid is absorbed. Let cool 15 minutes and serve warm with Cinnamon Spiced "Cream," page 165 (optional) or cover tightly and refrigerate 4 to 6 hours to serve it cold. Stored in a tightly covered container, leftover pudding will keep for 3 days.

Amount per serving, based on 6 servings: 172 Calories; 1g Fat; 0g Saturated fat; 3g Protein; 12mg Sodium; 38g Total Carbohydrate; 15g Sugars; 2g Fiber

Oh yeah! These delectable little cuties are so simple to make, you just may want to make a double batch. With only four ingredients, you can't go wrong with this easy twist on a classic cookie.

Four-Ingredient Chocolate Chip Oatmeal Cookies

EASE FACTOR   MAKES 16 TO 18 COOKIES

2 large, ripe bananas

1¼ cups rolled oats

⅓ cup raisins

⅓ cup vegan dark chocolate chips

Preheat the oven 375 degrees F. Line a large baking sheet with unbleached parchment paper.

Put the bananas in a medium-sized bowl and mash with a potato masher or large fork until smooth. Add the oats, raisins and chocolate chips; stir to combine.

Using a cookie scoop or large spoon, drop a heaping tablespoonful of the cookie batter onto the lined baking sheet, gently flattening it with a rubber spatula or clean fingertips. Continue in this manner with the remaining cookie dough.

Bake for 13 to 17 minutes, or until the edges are golden brown and cookies are almost set. Transfer the cookies to a wire rack and let cool for 10 minutes. Stored in an airtight container in the refrigerator, cookies will keep for about 3 days.

Amount per serving, based on 1 cookie: 59 Calories; 2g Fat; 1g Saturated fat; 1g Protein; 1mg Sodium; 11g Total Carbohydrate; 4g Sugars; 2g Fiber

These delectable baked beauties are kept moist and juicy by wrapping them in parchment before baking. The result is a mouthwatering, healthy dessert that doubles as a breakfast treat!

Baked Apples in Parchment

EASE FACTOR ❷   MAKES 2 TO 3 SERVINGS

2 very large or 3 medium baking apples such as Rome Beauty or Jonagold

5 heaping tablespoons raisins

1 tablespoon chopped walnuts

2 teaspoons raw unsweetened shredded dried coconut

2 tablespoons maple syrup

Preheat the oven to 375 degrees F. Line a large loaf pan with unbleached parchment paper, leaving a 6-inch overhang of the paper on each of the long sides of the pan. Cut a ½-inch slice off the top (stem end) of each apple and set aside. Core the apples.

Put the raisins, walnuts, coconut and 2 teaspoons maple syrup in a small mixing bowl and stir to combine. Stuff each apple with the raisin filling, dividing it evenly between the apples. Brush the tops of the stuffing with the remaining maple syrup using a pastry brush or back of a small spoon. Replace the reserved tops of the apples. Carefully position the apples in the pan so they will remain upright while baking. Wrap the apples tightly in the parchment paper by pulling the excess paper over the apples and folding it together to firmly seal.

Bake for 45 to 50 minutes, or until the apples are soft and the filling is bubbly. Let stand 20 minutes before serving. Serve warm, or cover tightly, refrigerate 3 to 6 hours and serve cold.

Amount per serving, based on 3 servings: 142 Calories; 2g Fat; 1g Saturated fat; 1g Protein; 3mg Sodium; 33g Total Carbohydrate; 25g Sugars; 4g Fiber

EASE-Y TWO-INGREDIENT RECIPE

Slice organic apples, then slather them with peanut butter for a quick treat.

Need an impressive dessert for an elegant meal? These luscious confections will provide the perfect finish to your meal, prompting "oohs" and "ahs" from your guests.

fancy finishes

13

Facing page: Sweet Cocoa Cupcakes with Rich Chocolate Frosting, page 194

Deep Dark Chocolate Truffle Pudding

EASE FACTOR ①   **MAKES 6 TO 8 SERVINGS**

The title of this recipe says it all. Wow your guests with a pudding that tastes so decadent, they will not believe it's totally soy-free, gluten-free *and* vegan! Silky smooth, thick, rich and super chocolaty—this is a flawless dessert that will impress the chocolate fans in your life.

1 cup raw cashews

2 cups filtered or spring water

3 tablespoons Sucanat or brown sugar

1 tablespoon unsweetened cocoa powder

1 teaspoon vanilla extract

4 Medjool dates, pitted and chopped

1 cup vegan chocolate chips

Put the cashews and 1 cup water in a small bowl. Refrigerate and let soak for 3 to 4 hours. Drain the cashews and rinse well under cold-running water. Drain and rinse again.

Heat the remaining 1 cup water in a small saucepan over medium heat until steaming hot, but not boiling. Put the chilled, soaked cashews, Sucanat (or brown sugar), cocoa powder, vanilla extract, dates and chocolate chips in a blender container *in the order listed*. Pour in the steaming hot water and process until completely smooth.

Divide the mixture between six small wine glasses or eight espresso cups. Refrigerate 4 to 8 hours or until set. Serve chilled with Vegan Whipped Topping (page 201) spooned or piped on top, if desired.

Watch Laura Theodore make this recipe at vegan-ease.com

Amount per serving, based on 8 servings: 211 Calories; 11g Fat; 6g Saturated fat; 3g Protein; 1mg Sodium; 32g Total Carbohydrate; 26g Sugars; 3g Fiber

Rockin' Berry Parfaits

EASE FACTOR ❷   MAKES 6 SERVINGS

These bountiful parfaits are the perfect way to serve farm fresh strawberries, raspberries and blueberries when they are in season. A delectable cashew "cream" is layered between layers of luscious berries, garnished with a cookie on top. The red, white and blue theme of this dessert makes an excellent choice for a July 4th party. *Delightful!*

CASHEW-COCONUT "CREAM" LAYER

1½ cups raw cashews, soaked (see note)

¼ cup raw unsweetened shredded dried coconut, soaked (see note)

1 teaspoon vanilla extract

¾ cup filtered or spring water, plus more as needed

2 tablespoons maple syrup

BERRY LAYER

2 to 3 cups fresh raspberries or strawberries (de-stemmed and sliced), plus more for garnish

2 to 3 cups fresh blueberries, plus more for garnish

ADDITIONAL INGREDIENTS

3 vegan cookies, cut in half, for garnish

4 mint sprigs, for garnish

Put all of the Cashew-Coconut "Cream" ingredients in a blender and process until smooth and creamy. Add more water if needed to reach a whipped cream consistency. Refrigerate 2 to 4 hours, or until thoroughly chilled.

To assemble the parfaits (see note), put a heaping tablespoon or more of the "cream" in each of six parfait, wine or martini glasses. Top the "cream" with one-sixth of the raspberries or strawberries (reserving 6 pieces for garnish). Then top with another heaping tablespoon of "cream." Next, add one-sixth of the blueberries to each glass (reserving 6 blueberries for garnish). Spoon the remaining Cashew-Coconut "Cream" over the top of the parfaits, dividing it evenly among the six glasses. Garnish each parfait with one raspberry or a few strawberry pieces, one blueberry, a cookie half and a mint sprig. Serve immediately (see note).

Chef's Notes

- To soak the *cashews*, put them in a small bowl and pour in enough water to cover. Refrigerate 1 to 2 hours. Drain and rinse well under cool running water.

- To soak the *coconut*, put it in a small bowl and pour in enough water to cover. Refrigerate 1 to 2 hours. Drain well before use.

- The parfaits are best assembled right before serving but you may assemble them up to 1 hour in advance and keep refrigerated.

Amount per serving, based on 6 servings: 423 Calories; 27g Fat; 6g Saturated fat; 12g Protein; 41mg Sodium; 41g Total Carbohydrate; 19g Sugars; 8g Fiber

Blueberry Cheeze-Cake Squares

EASE FACTOR ③   MAKES 9 SQUARES

Here are nutritious ingredients disguised as a decadent, creamy dessert bar nestled in a tasty fruit and nut crust—all topped with fresh blueberries. These squares double as a delightful breakfast pastry, too!

CRUST

⅓ cup raisins

⅓ cup raw almonds

⅓ cup raw unsweetened shredded dried coconut

FILLING

1 block (14 to 16 ounces) extra-firm regular tofu

2 tablespoons maple syrup

1 teaspoon vanilla extract

TOPPING

3 heaping tablespoons apricot preserves mixed with 2 teaspoons water

1 cup fresh blueberries, washed and patted dry

Preheat oven to 375 degrees F.

To make the crust, put the raisins, almonds and coconut in a high-performance blending appliance and process into a smooth dough. Put the dough on a piece of parchment paper (on a solid surface) and place another piece of the parchment over the top of the dough. Using a rolling pin, flatten the dough into about an 8-inch square. Transfer the dough onto an ungreased, 8-inch square, nonstick baking pan. Press the dough mixture evenly into the bottom of the pan.

To make the filling, put the tofu, maple syrup and vanilla extract in a blender and process until smooth and creamy. Pour the tofu mixture over the crust. Spread in an even layer and smooth the top. Bake for 25 minutes, or until firm to the touch. Put the pan on a wire rack. Carefully run a table knife around the perimeter of the cheeze-cake to ensure it does not stick to the side of the pan.

Immediately spread the diluted apricot preserves evenly over the top of the cheeze-cake, using a pastry brush or small spoon. Arrange the blueberries in a pretty pattern on top of the preserves, pressing down lightly so they adhere. Cover the pan loosely and refrigerate 1 to 3 hours. Cut into 9 squares and serve. Stored in an airtight container in the refrigerator, leftover squares will keep for 24 hours.

Amount per serving, based on 9 servings: 161 Calories; 7g Fat; 1g Saturated fat; 8g Protein; 10mg Sodium; 18g Total Carbohydrate; 14g Sugars; 1g Fiber

Chocolate-Coconut Quick Cake

EASE FACTOR **2**   MAKES 10 SERVINGS

This recipe certainly takes the cake when you need a quick chocolate fix.
Serve it to your family and friends and they will surely ask for seconds.
(Just make sure you save yourself a nice big piece!)

CAKE

2 cups whole wheat flour

1½ teaspoons baking soda

⅛ teaspoon sea salt

½ cup raw unsweetened shredded dried coconut

½ cup unsweetened cocoa powder

1 cup brown sugar or Sucanat

1⅓ cups plus 3 tablespoons non-dairy milk

1 tablespoon apple cider vinegar

2 teaspoons vanilla extract

FROSTING

¾ cup vegan dark chocolate chips

TOPPINGS (OPTIONAL)

Sweet Cherry Compote (page 200)

Cashew-Tofu Dessert "Cream" (page 201)

Preheat the oven to 375 degrees F. Lightly coat a 9-inch round cake pan with vegan margarine.

Put the flour, baking soda and salt in a large bowl; stir with a dry whisk to combine. Add the coconut and cocoa powder; stir with the whisk to combine. Add the sugar and stir once more.

Stir in the nondairy milk, vinegar and vanilla, mixing just until incorporated.

Pour the batter into the prepared pan and smooth the top. Bake for 25 to 30 minutes, or until a toothpick inserted in the center of the cake comes out clean. Remove the cake from the oven and immediately sprinkle the chocolate chips evenly over the top of the piping hot cake. Put the cake back in the oven for 20 to 30 seconds to let the chips partially melt. Remove the cake from the oven. Working quickly, spread the melting chocolate chips evenly over the top of the cake, using an offset spatula or rubber spatula.

Put the pan on a wire rack and loosen the sides of the cake with a knife. Cool for 20 to 30 minutes before serving.

You may cut the cake right in the pan, or if desired, lift the whole cake out of the pan using two flat, flexible spatulas and place it on a serving platter. Serve with Sweet Cherry Compote (page 200) and/or Cashew-Tofu Dessert "Cream" (page 201) on the side (optional). Covered tightly and stored in the refrigerator, leftover cake will keep for about 3 days.

Amount per serving, based on 10 servings (without optional ingredients): 296 Calories; 11g Fat; 7g Saturated fat; 7g Protein; 27mg Sodium; 50g Total Carbohydrate; 23g Sugars; 8g Fiber

Sweet Cocoa Cupcakes with Rich Chocolate Frosting

EASE FACTOR ③

Oh wow—these cupcakes are amazing! That's what I said the first time I made these simple, but super tempting treats. Avocado and a light version of vegan "buttermilk" both stand in effortlessly for the butter and the egg, while tofu and dark vegan chocolate chips whip up to provide a rich and decadent frosting. So pretty too—a real crowd pleaser!

CUPCAKES

½ cup nondairy milk

1½ teaspoons freshly squeezed lemon juice

½ cup peeled, seeded and chopped avocado (1-inch chunks)

1 cup filtered or spring water, plus more as needed

1 cup plus 3 tablespoons whole wheat flour, plus more as needed

⅔ cup vegan white sugar

¼ cup plus 1½ tablespoons unsweetened cocoa powder

½ teaspoon baking powder

1 teaspoon vanilla extract

FROSTING

⅓ cup nondairy milk

8 to 10 ounces firm regular tofu

2 tablespoons vegan powdered sugar

⅓ heaping cup vegan chocolate chips

Preheat the oven to 375 degrees F. Line a six-cup standard muffin pan with paper liners.

Put ½ cup of nondairy milk and the lemon juice into a small bowl and stir to combine. Let the mixture stand for 5 to 10 minutes to make a light vegan "buttermilk."

Put the avocado and ½ cup water in a blender and process until smooth and creamy in texture.

Meanwhile, put the flour, sugar, cocoa powder and baking powder in a large bowl and stir with a dry whisk to combine. Stir in the avocado mixture, the "buttermilk" mixture, ½ cup water and vanilla extract.

The batter may be quite loose, but if it seems overly wet, stir in a bit more flour, 1 tablespoon at a time, until the mixture is moist but not runny. Alternately, if the batter seems overly dry, stir in a bit more water, 1 tablespoon at a time, until the mixture is moist.

Mound the mixture equally into the six lined cups. Bake for 35 minutes, or until set and a toothpick inserted in the middle of a cupcake comes out clean. Let cool for 10 minutes, then remove the cupcakes and put them on a wire rack. Cool completely before frosting the cupcakes.

Amount per serving, based on 6 servings: 212 Calories; 8g Fat; 3g Saturated fat; 10g Protein; 30mg Sodium; 32g Total Carbohydrate; 11g Sugars; 5g Fiber

While the cupcakes bake, heat ⅓ cup of non-dairy milk in a small saucepan over medium-low heat until steaming hot, but not boiling. Put the tofu, powdered sugar and chocolate chips in a blender. Pour in the steaming nondairy milk and process until smooth.

Put a piping bag that has been fitted with a star tip into a tall glass, so it remains upright. Spoon the frosting into the piping bag (see note). Refrigerate the frosting for 1 to 2 hours, or until it is thoroughly chilled and firm enough to pipe onto the cupcakes.

Once the cupcakes have cooled and the frosting is chilled, pipe a generous amount of frosting on top of each cupcake. Serve immediately, or place the cupcakes in a tightly covered container and refrigerate until serving. For best taste, remove the cupcakes from the refrigerator about 15 minutes before serving.

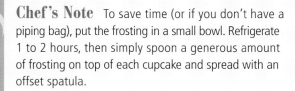

Chef's Note To save time (or if you don't have a piping bag), put the frosting in a small bowl. Refrigerate 1 to 2 hours, then simply spoon a generous amount of frosting on top of each cupcake and spread with an offset spatula.

Upside-Down Apple 'n Oat Mini-Cakes

EASE FACTOR ①   **MAKES 6 SERVINGS**

These supremely nutritious little cakes make a generous dessert—plus, they easily double as the perfect breakfast treat.

1 medium apple, cored and thinly sliced

2 tablespoons maple syrup

½ teaspoon ground cinnamon

2 cups sliced ripe bananas (2 large or 3 medium)

1 cup rolled oats

¼ cup plus 2 tablespoons raisins

¼ cup chopped walnuts

Preheat the oven to 375 degrees F. Liberally coat a six-cup jumbo muffin pan with vegan margarine.

Put the sliced apple, 1 tablespoon maple syrup and ¼ teaspoon cinnamon in a medium-sized bowl and stir to coat. Arrange one-sixth of the coated apple slices in the bottom of each of the six jumbo muffin cups.

Put the bananas and ¼ teaspoon cinnamon in a medium-sized bowl and mash until smooth, using a potato masher or large fork. Stir in the oats, raisins and walnuts. Spoon one-sixth of the oat mixture over the apple slices (filling the cups about two-thirds full) and smooth the tops, using a rubber spatula.

Bake for 25 to 30 minutes, or until firm to the touch and slightly golden. Put the pan on a wire rack and loosen the sides of each cake with a knife. Let cool for 5 minutes. Invert the pan onto the wire rack, releasing the cakes, apple side up. Brush the tops with the remaining 1 tablespoon maple syrup. Let cool for an additional 5 minutes. Serve warm or at room temperature.

Covered tightly and stored in the refrigerator, leftover cakes will keep for about 2 days.

Amount per serving, based on 6 servings: 192 Calories; 4g Fat; 0g Saturated fat; 4g Protein; 3mg Sodium; 35g Total Carbohydrate; 21g Sugars; 4g Fiber

Strawberry Mountain Pie

This delightful and delicious pie provides the perfect showcase for seasonal organic strawberries. The filling is *so* creamy you will not believe it's based in raw cashews and tofu. Easy to assemble and super yummy!

CRUST

1 cup plus 2 tablespoons vegan cookie crumbs or vegan graham cracker crumbs (see note)

3 to 5 heaping tablespoons sesame tahini

1½ tablespoons nondairy milk

FILLING

16 ounces extra-firm regular tofu

8 ounces soft silken tofu

⅓ cup raw cashews

⅓ cup plus 1 tablespoon vegan white sugar or your preferred dry sweetener

TOPPING

16 ounces organic strawberries

2 tablespoons strawberry preserves

2½ teaspoons filtered or spring water

Preheat the oven to 400 degrees F.

To make the crust, put the cookie crumbs, 3 heaping tablespoons tahini and 1½ tablespoons nondairy milk in a medium-sized bowl and combine using a large fork or dough blender. Add more tahini until the crumbs are moistened, but still crumbly in texture (up to 5 heaping tablespoons of tahini in all). Press the crumb mixture evenly into the bottom of a 9-inch pie plate. Bake for 5 minutes. Put the pie plate on a wire rack and let cool for 10 minutes.

While the crust cools, put the extra-firm regular tofu, silken tofu, cashews and sugar in a blender and process until smooth. Pour the tofu mixture over the cooled crust. Spread in an even layer and smooth the top. Bake for 20 to 30 minutes, or until the top of the pie is slightly firm to the touch (center of the filling will still be very soft). Put the pan on a wire rack and let cool 5 minutes.

Amount per serving, based on 8 servings: 166 Calories; 6g Fat; 1g Saturated fat; 7g Protein; 57mg Sodium; 23g Total Carbohydrate; 12g Sugars; 2g Fiber

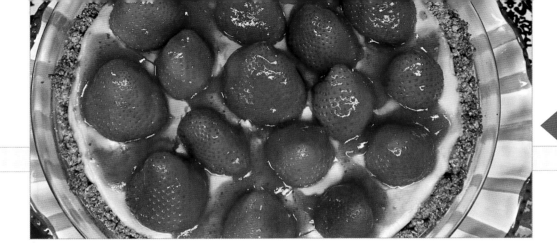

While the pie bakes, trim ⅛- to ¼-inch off the wide end of each strawberry. Then, when the pie is out of the oven but still warm, arrange the strawberries, flat end down, in a pleasing pattern on top of the pie, gently pressing the end of each strawberry into the filling so it stands upright. Put the preserves and water in a small mixing bowl and whisk together. Spread the preserves evenly over the top of the strawberries using a pastry brush or small spoon.

Refrigerate 4 to 8 hours before serving. Carefully cut the pie into slices (the filling will be soft). Stored tightly covered in the refrigerator, leftover pie will keep for about 2 days.

> **Chef's Note** To make cookie crumbs, put 1½ to 2 cups of broken-up vegan cookies in a blender, and process to coarse crumbs. Add more cookies, as needed, to make the amount of crumbs needed for this recipe.

VEGAN-*EASE*-Y TIP

I buy bags of organic frozen raspberries, blueberries, and strawberries at my supermarket. I keep them on hand to use when I am making smoothies or creamy frozen desserts.

Sweet Cherry Compote

EASE FACTOR ❶

Another contribution by Tara, our *Jazzy Vegetarian* sous chef, this lovely cherry sauce makes a delightful companion to a chocolate or vanilla cake. Delicious as a colorful and tasty topper to nondairy frozen desserts, too.

4 cups frozen sweet cherries

½ cup apple cider

6 tablespoons vegan sugar

Put all of the ingredients in a small saucepan and stir to combine. Bring to a boil over medium-high heat, stirring frequently. Decrease the heat to low and simmer for 50 to 60 minutes, stirring occasionally, until the cherries have begun to breakdown and the liquid has thickened. Remove from the heat and let cool before serving.

Amount per serving, based on 10 servings: 40 Calories; 0g Fat; 0g Saturated fat; 0g Protein; 1mg Sodium; 9g Total Carbohydrate; 8g Sugars; 1g Fiber

Cashew-Tofu Dessert "Cream"

EASE FACTOR **1**

This blend of cashews and tofu produces a silky, smooth texture and mouthwatering taste. Use this vegan cream in place of dairy cream in many recipes, or as a topper for your favorite fresh fruit, cake or pie.

1½ cups whole, raw cashews, soaked (see note)

¾ block (10 to 12 ounces), firm regular or silken tofu

½ cup filtered or spring water, plus more as needed

5 tablespoons maple syrup, plus more as needed

Amount per serving, based on 10 servings: 146 Calories; 9g Fat; 1g Saturated fat; 6g Protein; 8mg Sodium; 12g Total Carbohydrate; 7g Sugars; 1g Fiber

Put all of the ingredients in a blender and process until smooth. Add more water if needed to reach a whipped cream consistency. Taste and add more maple syrup, if desired. Refrigerate 2 to 4 hours, or until thoroughly chilled.

Chef's Note To soak the cashews, put them in a small bowl and pour in water to cover. Cover and refrigerate 1 to 4 hours. Drain and rinse well under cool running water. The cashews are now ready to use in this recipe.

Vegan Whipped Topping

EASE FACTOR **1**

When you need a really quick dessert topping, this thick and tantalizing "cream" fills the bill. Whips up in five minutes flat.

1 cup raw cashews

¼ cup nondairy milk

1 teaspoon vanilla extract

3 tablespoons maple syrup

Put all of the ingredients in a blender and process until smooth. Stored tightly covered in the refrigerator, this "cream" will keep up to 2 days.

Amount per serving, based on 8 servings: 179 Calories; 13g Fat; 2g Saturated fat; 5g Protein; 6mg Sodium; 14g Total Carbohydrate; 6g Sugars; 1g Fiber

Hosting family celebrations and seasonal parties during the holidays can be challenging, but serving a delicious feast that everyone will appreciate is made easier with this chapter.

stress-free holiday recipes

14

Facing page: Chocolate Party Parfaits with Mocha "Cream," page 220

Cranberry lovers rejoice! Equally tart and sweet, this cake makes a spectacular holiday morning treat that's surprisingly easy to make. The tantalizing tang of fresh red cranberries juxtaposed with a moist, semi-sweet, orange juice-laced cake serves colorful double duty as a dessert—just add a sprinkle of vegan powdered sugar and serve nondairy frozen "ice cream" on the side. *Deck the halls!*

Cranberry Christmas Coffee Cake

EASE FACTOR ❷   **MAKES 8 SERVINGS**

2 cups fresh cranberries

1 tablespoon maple syrup

1½ cups whole wheat flour

2 teaspoons baking powder

¼ teaspoon sea salt

½ cup firmly packed brown sugar

3 tablespoons ground flaxseeds

1½ cups orange juice

½ cup chopped walnuts

Preheat the oven to 350 degrees F. Lightly spread vegan margarine over the sides of a 9-inch round baking pan and line the bottom with unbleached parchment paper.

Put the cranberries and maple syrup in a medium-sized bowl and gently stir to coat evenly. Arrange the cranberries in a single layer in the bottom of the prepared pan.

To make the cake, put the flour, baking powder and salt in a large bowl and stir with a dry whisk to combine. Add the brown sugar and ground flaxseeds; stir with the whisk to combine. Add the orange juice and stir just until evenly incorporated and smooth. Add the walnuts and stir just until combined.

Pour the mixture into the prepared pan and smooth the top. Bake for 45 to 50 minutes, or until the top is golden and firm and a toothpick inserted in the center comes out clean.

Put the pan on a wire rack and loosen the sides with a knife. Let cool for 15 minutes. Invert onto a serving platter and very carefully peel off the parchment paper. Let cool for 10 to 15 minutes before slicing. Serve warm or at room temperature. Wrapped tightly and refrigerated, leftover cake will keep for about 3 days.

Amount per serving, based on 8 servings: 236 Calories; 7g Fat; 1g Saturated fat; 5g Protein; 6mg Sodium; 41g Total Carbohydrate; 22g Sugars; 5g Fiber

This attractive casserole features eggless "eggs" and hearty potatoes, making an excellent holiday breakfast or substantial brunch entrée to serve to vegans and omnivores alike. It's the perfect solution for serving an early day meal to overnight guests that you'd like to impress. It has a fairly long list of ingredients but takes only about 15 minutes to assemble for the oven.

Festive Breakfast Casserole

EASE FACTOR **2**   MAKES 4 TO 6 SERVINGS

2½ teaspoons extra-virgin olive oil

3 medium russet potatoes, baked, chilled and cut in ¼-inch slices (see note, page 158)

½ teaspoon sea salt

½ teaspoon smoked paprika

2 cups lightly packed baby spinach, washed and dried

1 block (14 to 16 ounces) extra-firm regular tofu

1 teaspoon reduced-sodium tamari

1 teaspoon dried oregano

½ teaspoon ground turmeric

⅛ teaspoon cayenne pepper

1 medium sweet red pepper, chopped

⅔ cup fresh flat leaf parsley, chopped

1 cup shredded vegan cheese (optional)

Preheat the oven to 400 degrees F. Lightly coat the bottom and sides of a medium-sized casserole with ½ teaspoon olive oil. Arrange ½ of the potato slices in a single layer in the bottom of the casserole. Sprinkle ¼ teaspoon of salt and ¼ teaspoon of smoked paprika evenly over the potatoes. Arrange all of the baby spinach in an even layer over the potatoes.

Put the tofu, tamari, oregano, turmeric and cayenne pepper in a medium-sized bowl and mash with a potato masher or large fork until the mixture resembles scrambled eggs. Spread the tofu mixture in an even layer on top of the spinach, patting it down slightly with a rubber spatula.

Arrange the remaining potato slices in a single layer over the tofu. Brush the potatoes with 2 teaspoons olive oil, then sprinkle ¼ teaspoon of salt and ¼ teaspoon of smoked paprika evenly over the potatoes. Arrange the chopped sweet red pepper over the potato slices in an even layer and then sprinkle the parsley over the top of the casserole.

Cover tightly and bake for 50 minutes. Uncover and spread the vegan cheese in the center of the casserole, if desired, leaving a 1-inch border of the red peppers and parsley around the perimeter of the casserole. Bake uncovered for 8 to 10 minutes, or until the "cheese" is melted and edge of casserole is golden brown. Put the casserole on a wire rack and let cool 10 to 15 minutes before serving.

Amount per serving, based on 6 servings: 153 Calories; 4g Fat; 1g Saturated fat; 9g Protein; 77mg Sodium; 22g Total Carbohydrate; 3g Sugars; 3g Fiber

Nutritional Information with optional vegan cheese: Amount per serving, based on 6 servings: 213 Calories; 8g Fat; 2g Saturated fat; 9g Protein; 244mg Sodium; 27g Total Carbohydrate; 3g Sugars; 4g Fiber

"What is this?" That's what I get asked at the check-out counter of my supermarket every time I purchase jicama. If you have been passing by this unfamiliar delicacy, shunning its odd shape and rough outer skin, here's the perfect opportunity to showcase this sweet and crunchy veggie in a happy holiday salad!

Zippy Jicama and Spinach Salad

EASE FACTOR **2**

10 ounces baby spinach, washed and dried

1 large jicama, washed, peeled and cut into strips

16 grape or cherry tomatoes, cut in half

12 pitted green or Kalamata olives, chopped

8 teaspoons chopped walnuts

4 teaspoons raw or roasted sunflower seeds

Creamy Dijon Dressing (page 101) or your preferred dressing

To make the salad, divide the baby spinach among four salad plates. For each serving, top with one-quarter of the jicama strips, 8 tomato halves and one-quarter of the chopped olives. Sprinkle each salad with 2 teaspoons of chopped walnuts and 1 teaspoon of sunflower seeds. Drizzle 1 tablespoon of dressing over each salad, plus more if desired. Serve immediately.

Amount per serving, based on 4 servings: 206 Calories; 7g Fat; 0g Saturated fat; 6g Protein; 431mg Sodium; 32g Total Carbohydrate; 6g Sugars; 17g Fiber

I first made these delicious peppers for a New Year's Eve party and they were a huge hit! Featuring a meaty-tasting seitan and hearty brown rice stuffing, these beautiful bells satiate omnivores and vegans alike. Ready for the oven in under 20 minutes, these six-ingredient wonders are equally ideal for a holiday party or weeknight supper.

Stuffed Green Bell Peppers

EASE FACTOR ❷   MAKES 6 SERVINGS

6 medium green bell peppers

1 jar (about 28 ounces) vegan marinara sauce

2 teaspoons extra-virgin olive oil (optional)

2 packages (16 ounces) Italian flavored crumbled or ground seitan (see note)

2 cups cooked and cooled long-grain brown rice (see note)

2 teaspoons all-purpose seasoning blend

Chef's Notes

- You may use unflavored, ground seitan in place of the Italian flavored variety. If using unflavored seitan, add an additional heaping teaspoon of all-purpose seasoning or Italian seasoning blend to the filling mixture before stuffing the peppers.

- You may pre-cook the rice up to 48 hours ahead of making this recipe. Store it tightly covered in the refrigerator until use.

P reheat the oven to 400 degrees F. Slice about one inch off the top of each pepper. Seed the peppers.

Spread 1½ cups of the marinara sauce and the 2 teaspoons of olive oil (optional) evenly over the bottom of a casserole that's large and deep enough to hold all the peppers snugly so they remain upright during baking.

Put the seitan, brown rice and all-purpose seasoning in a large bowl and stir well until combined. Stir in ⅔ cup marinara sauce and mix to combine. Spoon one-sixth of the seitan mixture into each pepper, mounding it, if necessary. Spoon 2 heaping teaspoons of the marinara sauce over each pepper. Carefully position the peppers in the casserole so they will remain upright while baking.

Cover and bake for 50 to 60 minutes, or until the sauce is bubbly and the peppers are tender but not mushy. Let cool for 7 to 10 minutes before serving.

Serve the peppers with *tricolore* pasta on the side and topped with some of the sauce that has accumulated at the bottom of the casserole. Put the remaining sauce in a gravy boat or small bowl to pass around at the table.

Amount per serving, based on 6 servings: 307 Calories; 6g Fat; 0g Saturated fat; 24g Protein; 868mg Sodium; 40g Total Carbohydrate; 2g Sugars; 2g Fiber

Stuffed Green Bell Peppers, *above*   Butternut Squash Stuffed with Apples and Cranberries, *page 214, below*

In the northeast, late fall at the farm market brings many enticing kinds of squash. Butternut is one of my favorite varieties of winter squash to cook with because of its nutty sweetness. Stuffed with a savory and sweet blend of rice, spinach, apples, walnuts and cranberries, this cold weather seasonal dish makes a festive, nutritious and appealing entrée for any special meal.

Butternut Squash Stuffed with Apples and Cranberries

EASE FACTOR ②   MAKES 4 SERVINGS

1 very large butternut squash, peeled

2 cups cooked short-grain brown rice

1½ cups lightly packed baby spinach

1 medium apple, peeled, cored and diced

¼ cup dried cranberries

¼ cup finely chopped walnuts

1 teaspoon all-purpose seasoning blend

½ teaspoon sea salt

¼ teaspoon ground cinnamon

Preheat the oven to 375 degrees F. Line a large casserole dish with unbleached parchment paper.

Cut 2 to 3 inches off the top of the squash. Cut the squash in half *lengthwise* and then cut each piece in half *lengthwise* to make 4 sections of squash, equal in size. Scrape out the seeds from each section.

Put the rice, spinach, apple, cranberries, walnuts, all-purpose seasoning, sea salt and ground cinnamon in a medium-sized bowl and stir to combine. Divide the stuffing mixture evenly, mounding it into the hollowed center in each of the four squash pieces, mounding it as you go (see note).

Put the squash quarters, stuffing side up, in the prepared casserole dish. Tent with foil and bake for 1 to 1½ hours, or until the squash is very soft. For a crisp topping, remove the foil for the last 10 minutes of baking. Let cool 10 to 15 minutes and serve.

 Chef's Note If you end up with extra stuffing, put it in a small, covered casserole and bake alongside the squash like a holiday stuffing. Makes a great side dish.

 Watch Laura Theodore make this recipe at vegan-ease.com

Amount per serving, based on 4 servings: 332 Calories; 6g Fat; 1g Saturated fat; 9g Protein; 35mg Sodium; 70g Total Carbohydrate; 17g Sugars; 11g Fiber

Apples and sweet potatoes pair beautifully with the color, texture and tang of cranberries. This appetizing casserole can be assembled well ahead of time, making it ideal party fare either at home or as a pot-luck offering.

Cranberry, Apple and Sweet Potato Casserole

EASE FACTOR   **MAKE 6 SERVINGS**

2 large sweet potatoes, peeled and cut into ⅛- to ¼-inch slices

5 tablespoons maple syrup

2 teaspoons ground cinnamon

½ teaspoon extra-virgin olive oil (optional)

2 large red delicious apples, cored and cut into ½-inch slices

1 tablespoon freshly squeezed lemon juice

½ cup dried cranberries

Preheat the oven to 375 degrees F. Lightly oil an 11 x 8-inch or similar size casserole dish. Put the sweet potato slices, 2 tablespoons maple syrup, 1 teaspoon cinnamon and ½ teaspoon olive oil (optional) in a large bowl and stir with a large spoon to coat evenly. Arrange the sweet potato slices in overlapping layers in the prepared dish. Put the apple slices, lemon juice, 1 tablespoon maple syrup and 1 teaspoon cinnamon in the same large bowl and stir with a large spoon, coating evenly. Arrange the apples in overlapping layers on top of the sweet potatoes.

Put the cranberries and 1 tablespoon maple syrup in the same large bowl and stir with a large spoon to coat evenly. Scatter the cranberry mixture over the top of the apples. Cover and bake for 30 minutes. Remove from oven, uncover and drizzle the remaining 1 tablespoon of maple syrup over the top. Cover and bake for 30 to 40 minutes more, or until the sweet potatoes and apples are slightly caramelized, tender and browning around the edges. Let cool for 10 to 15 minutes. Serve warm.

Amount per serving, based on 6 servings: 151 Calories; 1g Fat; 0g Saturated fat; 1g Protein; 16mg Sodium; 38g Total Carbohydrate; 27g Sugars; 4g Fiber

EASE-Y TWO-INGREDIENT RECIPE

Bake a sweet potato and top it with canned lentil or black bean soup.

Just three ingredients make this holiday staple an easy side dish to serve any time of year. The maple syrup helps to caramelize the Brussels sprouts as they roast, while chili powder adds a touch of subtle heat. Bonus: This dish is ready for the oven in less than five minutes.

Chili-Maple Brussels Sprouts

EASE FACTOR   MAKES 4 SERVINGS

24 ounces Brussels sprouts, washed, trimmed and cut in half

2 tablespoons maple syrup

2 teaspoons chili powder

Preheat the oven to 375 degrees F. Line a large, rimmed baking pan with unbleached parchment paper.

Put all of the ingredients in a medium-sized bowl. Toss gently until the Brussels sprouts are evenly coated. Spread the Brussels sprouts in an even layer in the prepared pan. Roast for 30 to 35 minutes, or until soft and golden brown around the edges, turning once while cooking. Serve warm.

Amount per serving, based on 4 servings: 99 Calories; 1g Fat; 0g Saturated fat; 6g Protein; 43mg Sodium; 22g Total Carbohydrate; 10g Sugars; 6g Fiber

These little darlings are a fun and flavorful way to present potatoes. The inside pulp stays nice and tender while the outside gets crispy. Serve these on the side for any party meal, even breakfast!

Holiday Rosemary Smashed Potatoes

EASE FACTOR ❷   MAKES 6 TO 8 SERVINGS

35 to 40 ounces fingerling or baby potatoes, scrubbed

1½ tablespoons extra-virgin olive oil

1 tablespoon crushed dried rosemary

½ teaspoon sea salt, plus more as needed

 it a steamer basket into a medium-sized sauce-pan with a tight-fitting lid. Add 2 to 3 inches of cold water to the pot and then add the potatoes. Cover and bring to a boil. Steam the potatoes for 10 minutes. Transfer the potatoes to a large bowl and let cool 10 minutes.

While the potatoes cool, preheat the oven to 375 degrees F. Line a large, rimmed baking sheet with unbleached parchment paper.

Add the olive oil, rosemary and sea salt to the cooled potatoes and toss to lightly coat, using a large spoon, letting the excess olive oil and rosemary run to the bottom of the bowl. Arrange the potatoes about ½-inch apart in a single layer on the prepared baking sheet. Using a sturdy, flat spatula, "smash" each potato so it is slightly flattened. Brush the tops of the flattened potatoes with the seasoned oil that settled into the bottom of the mixing bowl.

Roast for 50 to 60 minutes, or until the potatoes are golden brown and slightly crispy. Season with more sea salt, if desired, while still hot. Let cool 10 minutes and serve warm.

Amount per serving, based on 8 servings: 139 Calories; 3g Fat; 0g Saturated fat; 3g Protein; 8mg Sodium; 25g Total Carbohydrate; 0g Sugars; 2g Fiber

These divinely rich parfaits make a glorious finish to any holiday meal. Serve this festive dessert at your soirée and your guests will be begging for the recipe!

Chocolate Party Parfaits with Mocha "Cream"

EASE FACTOR ❷   **MAKES 6 SERVINGS**

COOKIE LAYER

6 tablespoons cookie crumbs (see note)

CHOCOLATE LAYER

⅓ cup vanilla flavored nondairy milk

7 to 8 ounces (about ½ block) **firm regular tofu, drained**

1 bar (3.5 ounces) **vegan dark chocolate, finely chopped** (snack bar; not unsweetened baking chocolate)

MOCHA "CREAM" LAYER

2 tablespoons cold, strongly brewed coffee

2 tablespoons maple syrup

7 to 8 ounces (about ½ block) firm regular tofu, drained

2 heaping tablespoons Chocolate Layer mixture (above)

GARNISH

3 whole vegan cookies, cut in half

Put 1 tablespoon of the cookie crumbs in the bottom of six mini parfait glasses, wine glasses, or small dessert dishes.

To make the chocolate layer, heat the nondairy milk in a small saucepan over medium-low heat until steaming hot, but not boiling. *In this order*, put ½ block tofu in a blender and top with the chopped chocolate. Pour in the steaming hot nondairy milk and process until completely smooth. Spoon the chocolate mixture over the cookie crumbs, dividing it evenly among the parfait glasses, reserving 2 heaping tablespoons to use in the mocha "cream" layer.

Amount per serving, based on 6 servings: 165 Calories; 10g Fat; 3g Saturated fat; 5g Protein; 66mg Sodium; 15g Total Carbohydrate; 9g Sugars; 1g Fiber

To make the mocha "cream" layer, put the cold coffee, maple syrup, ½ block tofu and reserved 2 heaping tablespoons of the chocolate mixture in a blender and process until smooth. Spoon the mocha layer over the chocolate layer in the parfait glasses.

Refrigerate 4 to 6 hours, or until thoroughly chilled. Serve cold, garnished with half of a vegan cookie tucked into the center of the parfait.

Chef's Note To make cookie crumbs, put 2 or 3 vegan cookies in a blender, and process to coarse crumbs.

This delicate yet rich-tasting cake makes the perfect dessert for any winter holiday event. Served with a generous dollop of Vegan Whipped Topping (page 201), this cheeze-cake will be dressed to impress!

Pumpkin Spice Cheeze-Cake

EASE FACTOR **3**   **MAKES 8 TO 10 SERVINGS**

CRUST

1¾ cups cookie crumbs (ginger cookies work well)

¼ cup vegan margarine, melted

FILLING

2 tablespoons rolled oats

14 to 16 ounces firm regular tofu

1 can (about 16 ounces) unsweetened pumpkin purée

⅔ cup dark brown sugar

1 teaspoon vanilla extract

1 teaspoon ground cinnamon

¼ teaspoon allspice

TOPPING

3 tablespoons cookie crumbs

Preheat the oven to 350 degrees F. Liberally coat a 10-inch round springform pan with vegan margarine.

To make the crust, put 1¾ cups cookie crumbs and the melted margarine in a medium-sized bowl and mix with a fork until well combined. Pat the crumbs firmly into the bottom of the prepared pan. Bake the crust for 5 minutes. Remove from the oven and let cool 5 minutes.

To make the filling, put the rolled oats in a blender and process into coarse crumbs. Add the tofu, pumpkin purée, brown sugar, vanilla extract, cinnamon and allspice and process until smooth and creamy.

Pour the filling into the crust and bake for 30 to 35 minutes, or until firm to the touch. Remove the cake from the oven and place it on a wire rack. Cool for 15 minutes, then carefully run a table knife around the perimeter of the cake to ensure it does not stick to the side of the pan.

Sprinkle 3 tablespoons of cookie crumbs evenly over the top of the cake, gently pressing them into the top, so the crumbs adhere. Release the side of the springform pan to unmold.

Cover the cake very loosely and refrigerate 3 to 24 hours before serving. Serve with Vegan Whipped Topping (page 201) on the side, if desired. Covered tightly and stored in the refrigerator, leftover cheeze-cake will keep for about 2 days.

Amount per serving, based on 10 servings: 154 Calories; 7g Fat; 1g Saturated fat; 5g Protein; 62mg Sodium; 20g Total Carbohydrate; 15g Sugars; 2g Fiber

Not quite a cookie nor a candy, these not-too-sweet treats offer a creamy and chunky texture—the best of both worlds!

Merry Mocha Snowballs

EASE FACTOR ②   MAKES 18 TO 20 BALLS

COATING

⅓ cup plus 2 tablespoons raw unsweetened shredded dried coconut

CHOCOLATE MIXTURE

¼ cup plus 2 tablespoons nondairy milk

3 tablespoons strongly brewed coffee (see note)

1½ cups dark vegan chocolate chips

2 tablespoons raw unsweetened shredded dried coconut

½ teaspoon ground cinnamon

⅔ cup brown rice crisps (as found in crispy rice cereals)

Amount per serving, based on 1 servings/ball (based on 20 servings): 78 Calories; 6g Fat; 4g Saturated fat; 1g Protein; 7mg Sodium; 7g Total Carbohydrate; 0g Sugars; 3g Fiber

Line a medium-sized, rimmed baking pan with unbleached parchment paper. Put the coconut for coating the snowballs into a small bowl and set aside.

To make the chocolate mixture, put the nondairy milk and brewed coffee into a small saucepan and heat until simmering hot, but not boiling. Meanwhile, put the chocolate chips, 2 tablespoons coconut and cinnamon in a large bowl. Slowly pour half of the hot nondairy milk mixture over the top and stir slowly to start melting the chips. Pour the remaining hot nondairy milk mixture over the top and stir slowly to melt the remaining chips almost completely. Some chips will remain whole (this will provide the chunks). Gently fold in the rice crisps until they are incorporated.

Scoop up 1 tablespoon of the mixture and carefully form it into a ball. Roll the chocolate ball in the coconut until it is completely coated. Place it on the prepared baking pan. Repeat in the same manner with the remaining chocolate mixture to form 18 to 20 balls.

Refrigerate at least 30 minutes before serving. The balls may be made the day before or several hours in advance of serving. Thirty minutes prior to serving, remove the balls from the refrigerator, so they soften slightly.

Chef's Note To cut down on the caffeine, or for a kid-friendly version of this recipe, simply replace the 3 tablespoons of coffee with 3 tablespoons of maple syrup. Proceed as directed.

PART III

the menu, please!

Joyful Holiday Dinner

'Tis the season to eat jolly! Every year at holiday time, I reminisce about my childhood, when my mother and grandmother served delicious meals and sinfully scrumptious treats. If you, like so many of us, are serving a household of vegans, vegetarians and omnivores alike this year, here's an enchanting holiday menu to serve, savor and share throughout the merry season.

APPETIZERS

Mini Sweet Peppers with Hummus
PAGE 29

SOUP

Butternut Squash and Pear Bisque
PAGE 207

MAIN DISH

*Sunflower Seed, Cashew and Oat Loaf
with Mushroom-Basil Gravy*
PAGE 208

SIDE DISHES

Chili-Maple Brussels Sprouts
PAGE 216

Cranberry, Apple and Sweet Potato Casserole
PAGE 215

Holiday Rosemary Smashed Potatoes
PAGE 219

DESSERTS

Pumpkin Spice Cheeze-Cake
PAGE 222

Merry Mocha Snowballs
PAGE 224

acknowledgments

T his book could not have happened without the support, input and sheer passion of many people whom I thank with all my heart! First, my eternal gratitude goes to my husband and life-partner Andy—my rock!—whose daily support, love, pure faith in me (and continued eagerness to be my chief recipe tester) makes all the hard work worthwhile.

To my family and friends, I hope you know how much your encouragement has meant to me all these years. You have been my community, my village, and I have learned so much from your input and love.

Deep gratitude goes to my super-talented editor and dear friend Kit Emory without whose talent, understanding and ninja editing skills this book could not have happened! Likewise, I cannot thank enough the eagle-eyed Karen L. Stein for her extraordinary attention to detail in proofreading.

Thanks to Regina Eisenberg who has never wavered in her commitment to *Jazzy Vegetarian*, helping transform the television series from dream to reality. I am indebted to David Davis, Cheri Arbini, Kelsey Wallace and all of our team at *Oregon Public Broadcasting* for giving *Jazzy Vegetarian* a home on public television, and I gratefully appreciate Gayle Loeber and *NETA* for their excellent job in distributing the program.

Brava to Mitali Shah-Bixby for her superb work putting together the nutritional information for each recipe in this book. My deepest thanks to Julieanna Hever and Victoria Moran—our expert guests this season on *Jazzy Vegetarian*—who give the show extra pizzazz while imparting nutritional wisdom, and whose contributions to this book are truly invaluable.

Enormous gratitude abounds for John and Rhonda Wincek, the talented team who created such a vibrant design for the book, beautifully—and patiently—sorting out every detail along the way. And thank you to Tom Doherty and Ginger Bock at Cardinal Publishers Group for your great work in distributing *Vegan-Ease*, getting it on kitchen shelves nationwide! Thanks, also, to Roger Mohn at Versa Press, Inc., for working with us to print this book.

I am in awe of our conscientious, hard working, super-talented *Jazzy Vegetarian* television crew. Thank you, David Kaplan, Jacob

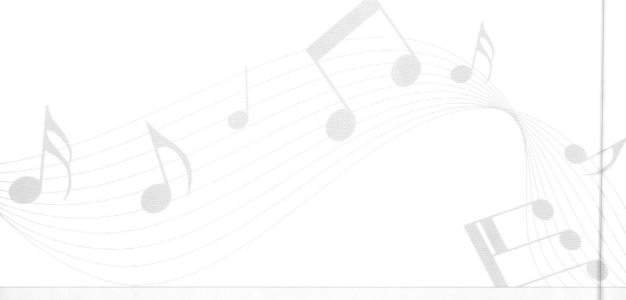

Fisher, Amy Marie McGowen, Tara Ciannella and George Ellis for exhibiting commitment and grace under pressure during a tight filming schedule. To the *Sub-Zero and Wolf Showroom* team, thanks for allowing us to film this season at your state-of-the-art facility.

Heartfelt thanks to my pal, the brilliantly talented and super-cool Rickey Medlocke, for flying to New York in -4 degree weather to appear on the show and for being an absolutely awesome and entertaining guest! Also, thanks to the Blackfoot Band, Eric and Al for coordinating the studio segments for that episode. *Mille grazie* to the fabulous Lidia Bastianich for taking time out of her super busy schedule to appear in Season Five, sharing her awesome knowledge of the vegetable kingdom and taking us to the wonderful world of *Eataly*.

I need to offer a jazzy shout-out to our PR pals Chris Roslan and Eileen Campion, along with a big thank you to Dianne Wenz for her support. Thanks, also, to Laura Cheadle and *Starving Artist Promotions* for helping to spread the word about *Vegan-Ease*! And a heart-filled thanks to my growing network of amazing vegan authors and bloggers Nava Atlas, Annie Oliverio, Rebecca Gilbert, Hannah Kaminsky, Jill McKeever and Zel Allen, for your continued support through the years. A special thank you goes to Purnima Schachter for her generous support in helping to make this book possible!

To the super talented Christina Pirello for inspiring vegan eating on public television when the task seemed impossible: Look at us now! To Farm Sanctuary and the tireless leadership of Gene Baur, eternal gratitude for dedicating your lives to the welfare of animals.

And, as always—to ALL of the animals on this Earth: This book is for *you*.

Above: Chocolate-Coconut Quick Cake, page 192

Jazzy Vegetarian
Lively Vegan Cuisine That's Easy and Delicious

Embrace healthful eating . . . one mouthwatering recipe at a time. In this companion cookbook to Season One of the popular public tele-

vision series, *Jazzy Vegetarian*, host Laura Theodore reveals how to create fabulous yet effortless plant-based recipes that will fit any need, whether you want to completely overhaul your diet or simply add a few exciting vegan dishes to your weekly repertoire. From Festive Lasagna, to Cashew French Toast, to chocolaty Pots De Crème, this cookbook contains all of the recipes from Season One and some of the recipes from Season Two featured in the series, plus many more. **All** *Jazzy Vegetarian* **recipes are vegan!**

$24.95 • 192 pages • hardcover • 8" x 9.5" • ISBN-13: 978-1570672613

Jazzy Vegetarian Classics
Vegan Twists on American Family Favorites

Classic American meals just became healthier and more delicious with Laura Theodore's vegan twist on traditional family fare. With over

150 quick-to-prepare and gourmet-style dishes, *Jazzy Vegetarian Classics* features Laura's creations, such as vegan Shish Kebabs, Burger and Fries, Spaghetti and "Wheatballs," and other spins on time-honored favorites, such as Black Forest Pecan Pie and Decadent Chocolate Ganache Cake. *Jazzy Vegetarian Classics* contains all of the recipes from Season Three and some of the recipes from Season Two and Season Four featured in the series, plus many more. **All** *Jazzy Vegetarian* **recipes are vegan!**

$26.95 • 312 pages • hardcover • 7" x 9.5" • ISBN-13: 978-1937856939

BY LAURA THEODORE

JAZZY VEGETARIAN DVDs

The Best of Jazzy Vegetarian 3-DISC, DVD Collection

Fans of this highly successful *Jazzy Vegetarian* series know that vegan chef Laura Theodore can turn any meal into a delicious special occasion. Each half-hour episode includes hands-on instruction and tasty tips for seasoned cooks and newcomers alike. Laura creates mouthwatering entrées like Holiday Stuffing Casserole, Spaghetti and "Wheatballs," and Polenta Pizza. And when sweet treats are in order, Laura highlights decadent and rich-tasting desserts like Chocolate Cake, Luscious Carrot Cupcakes and Homemade Pumpkin Pie.

$19.95 • 3-disc DVD

To purchase autographed copies of Laura's Cookbooks or DVDs, go to:

jazzyvegetarian.com or **vegan-ease.com**

"*Laura Theodore's Vegan-Ease* is a fantastic resource for anyone who wants to eat delicious food and get healthy without putting too much time or money into it—and let's be honest, is there anyone out there who doesn't want this? If you think that nutrition, taste-factor, and ease can't all come in one package when it comes to food, this book will cause you to think again. Laura Theodore has put together a collection of helpful tips and tasty recipes that make plant-based eating easier than ever. Don't miss out on an opportunity to read and use this great book!"

Neal Barnard, MD, President,
Physicians Committee for Responsible Medicine

"With *Laura Theodore's Vegan-Ease*, you will find smart, simple, and readily accessible recipes that are at the same time wonderfully delicious. While having fun preparing and eating any of the many great-tasting dishes, you will also be serving the most sustainable, resource-efficient foods that are unquestionably the best choices for your own health and that of our planet. What I like most about this cookbook is that Laura has so thoughtfully packaged and presented us with one more compelling reason to eat only plant-based foods—she's made it . . . *Easy!*"

Dr. Richard A. Oppenlander, researcher, consultant,
and award-winning author of *Food Choice and
Sustainability* and *Comfortably Unaware*

"It's just this simple: Laura Theodore performs kitchen magic. Give her a few fresh, whole-food ingredients and she'll create healthy, colorful, and delicious recipes with her warm, approachable style and a minimum of fuss. Somehow—it's that culinary magic thing—Laura conjures incredible flavor and variety out of basic, readily available ingredients, so even the novice cook can serve up tasty meals that are sure to please omnivores, vegetarians, and vegans alike."

Annie Oliverio, food photographer, blogger, and author
of *Crave Eat Heal: Plant-Based, Whole Food Recipes
to Satisfy Every Appetite*

"*Laura Theodore's Vegan-Ease* proves that anyone, anywhere, can cook mouth-watering vegan dishes using easy-to-find, inexpensive ingredients. This book is a must-have for anyone who wants to save time and money while cooking healthy meals that the whole family will love."

Dianne Wenz, vegan health and lifestyle coach,
DiannesVeganKitchen.com

"What a gorgeous book this is, with recipes that even I can do! As a performer, I am always looking to improve my diet to stay strong and healthy, and Laura gives me all the tools I need to make that happen. From helping me set up my kitchen to showing me how to make delicious, great-looking food, *Vegan-Ease* is preparing me for my next gig. Laura, you are a Rockstar!"

Karen Mason, Broadway star
(*Sunset Boulevard, Mamma Mia!*) and cabaret artist

"We wish this book had existed when we first went vegan. It not only makes adopting a plant-based diet a no-brainer, but Laura's mix of personal anecdotes, along with tried and true tips for the veg-curious, brings a sense of fun to the journey in a way only the *Jazzy Vegetarian* herself can do. With *Laura Theodore's Vegan-Ease*, you will be gently guided through the process of embracing a new way of eating by a true leader in the field of cooking."

Jasmin Singer, Executive Director, and
Mariann Sullivan, Program Director, *Our Hen House*

"*Laura Theodore's Vegan-Ease* gracefully dispels the most persistent myths about plant-based meals, proving that they're not time-consuming, expensive, or overly exotic. What she does prove is that enjoying vegan food is easy, delicious, and incredibly satisfying. With tips to get you started and delectable, do-able recipes for every meal of the day—*Vegan-Ease* is a go-to book, no matter where you are on the plant-based journey."

Nava Atlas, author of *Wild About Greens*
and *Vegan Holiday Kitchen*

"Laura simplifies the cooking process with sections on kitchen tools, pantry must-haves, company dinner menus, and even healthy clean-up tips. She makes it simple for novice and experienced chefs alike to prepare delicious, nutritious, and healthy vegan meals every day!"

Rebecca Gilbert, founder of the *Yummy Plants
Vegan Community* and author of *It's Easy to Start Eating Vegan*

"Virtuoso of the vegan kitchen, *Laura Theodore's Vegan-Ease* reaches a new high note with recipes that, while simple, radiate a full concert of flavor."

Daniel A. Nadeau, MD, author of *The Color Code,
A Revolutionary Eating Plan for Optimum Health*